The Q Guide to

Oscar® Parties and other award shows

The Q Guides

FROM ALYSON BOOKS

LIFESTYLE

Q

OUT THERE

GUIDE

The Q Guide to

Oscar® Parties and other award shows

Stuff You Didn't Even Know You Wanted to Know...about hosting a party your friends will talk about all year long

[**joel perry**]

alyson books
NEW YORK

THIS TRADE PAPERBACK ORIGINAL IS PUBLISHED BY
ALYSON BOOKS
P.O. BOX 1253
OLD CHELSEA STATION
NEW YORK, NEW YORK 10113-1251

DISTRIBUTION IN THE UNITED KINGDOM BY
TURNAROUND PUBLISHER SERVICES
UNIT 3, OLYMPIA TRADING ESTATE
COBURG ROAD, WOOD GREEN
LONDON 722 6TZ UNITED KINGDOM.

FIRST EDITION: JANUARY 2007

06 07 08 09 10 **a** 10 9 8 7 6 5 4 3 2 1

ISBN-10 1-55583-988-6
ISBN-13 978-1-55583-988-8

LIBRARY OF CONGRESS
CATALOGING-IN-PUBLICATION DATA IS ON FILE.

BOOK DESIGN BY VICTOR MINGOVITS

To Fred, the best prize I ever won

"I want you to have a party and be gay. *Very, very gay!*"

—BETTE DAVIS as the oh-so-brave
Judith Traherne in 1939's *Dark Victory*
(nominated for Best Actress…but didn't win)

Contents

Introduction: Why We're All Here for Oscar

"Good evening, Hollywood phonies."

—Chevy Chase, opening as host of the 60th Annual Academy Awards®

IS THERE anything more glorious, useless, brilliant, crapridden, inspiring, and thrilling than the movies? They give us dreams, expose our fears, present our zeitgeist, and take up far too much of our conversation in relation to what's really important. But what *is* really more important in these scary times than occasionally shutting out the news and getting into a screaming, dialogue-quoting bitch-fight over how the hell Nicole Kidman won the Oscar for *The Hours* over Renée Zelwegger in *Chicago*. (Of course we all know it was because Renée's character didn't kill herself—oh, you haven't seen *The Hours*? Pity.)

In fact there can be only one thing more important: throwing an Oscar party to celebrate it!

The very fact that you picked up this book means you're passionate about movies, prizes, and parties, and that makes you my kind of people. So I want to help you enjoy the hell out of that by providing you with the world's best guide to throwing an Oscar party. If, for some reason, you wish to throw a party for the Emmys, Grammys, Golden Globes, or Tony Awards, hooray for you! We'll get into that, too. But you should still read all about throwing your very own Oscar-fest because, let's face it, the Academy Awards are the Mother of All Awards Shows. Everything you do for those other awards is based on what you could (and should!) be doing for Oscar.

QUOTE

"As you all know by now, this is the 51st Annual Academy Awards. Two hours of sparkling entertainment, spread out over a four-hour show."

—Johnny Carson, hosting the 51st Annual Academy Awards

The annual awards of the Academy of Motion Picture Arts and Sciences are the Gay Super Bowl where anything can happen. Many straight people, goddess love 'em, just don't get the Oscars. With depressing frequency they also don't get parties. That's why the universe made gay people. And if you're a straight person who "accidentally" wandered into the homo corner of your local bookstore, don't worry, because I'm going to share all our party-throwing secrets with you. After one of these parties, people are going to treat you like us: seeking you out for the best gossip, asking your opinion on shoes (sensible or otherwise), and assuming you know Madonna personally. It's hilarious—you'll love it!

Getting Started Late?

While this book does include preparations that can start months prior to the Academy Awards show, there is no need to gnash your pearly teeth if you find yourself reading these words mere days before the telecast. There are plenty of ideas here just for you, too. All you need to do as you read is to keep in mind your time constraints. So you don't have time to redecorate your entire house to reflect a *Crouching Tiger, Hidden Dragon* theme? You can still have a great party and make your guests very happy with, say, Chinese takeout, swag bags full of fortune cookies, and one or two of the Oscar-viewing games and competitions described herein. The key is to:

1. Pick and choose what you can pull off.
2. Don't overreach and make yourself crazy.
3. Do what feels comfortable.

Your natural gifts for fun and enjoyment will carry the day. How do I know? Because you were fun enough to buy this book, which tells me you're darned serious about your partying.

But *next year* you can do it up right with all the bells and whistles.

"I know what you're thinking…Where's that big, terrible number that usually opens the Oscars?"

—Billy Crystal, hosting the 62nd Annual Academy Awards

Why Is This Night Different from All Other Nights?

The Academy Awards is the only awards show with the clout to get the stars out in (what their stylists consider) their finest, to get them to go on television and mangle their lines in front of a live international audience, and to risk being misidentified by Joan Rivers. ("It's F. Murray Abraham! What? It's Ben Kingsley? It looks exactly like F. Murray Abraham." Yeah? On what planet, Joan?)

Oscar night is the acme, the *n'est plus ultra*, the top horndog of all award shows. When it comes to fantasies, money, ego, storytelling, horrendous taste, stunning style, and glittering, glorious dysfunction, movies are simply the biggest game in town, period.

Besides, other awards shows simply do not hold a candle to them.

The Golden Globe® Awards?

The Golden Globes are a mishmash of television and movies, which, I'm sorry, is like mixing meat and dairy. They're also given out by foreigners who are still wandering around the U.S. going, "These Americans, they are so crazy-strange—oh, look, free booze!" And while the Golden Globes are always good for hoot-inspiring fashions and to help you handicap your Oscar ballot choices, they just don't have the *élan* or stratospheric excitement of the Academy Awards.

Something feels thrown together about handing out awards in the same space where, an hour earlier, the participants were all eating dinner. It's impossible to maintain a regal dignity where the house is filled with waiters busy keeping the champagne away from Courtney Love's table and shushing Charlie Sheen's "guest." After a few years the Oscars figured out that you should not dispense awards after a dinner of fatty beef and underdone chicken, and they moved out of the Roosevelt Hotel ballroom and into a theater. The Golden Globes have yet to catch on.

The Emmy® Awards?

At least the Emmys are held in a theater and not a hotel ballroom. Unfortunately, though, it remains about television. And the difference between cinema and television is the difference between *Titanic* and *The Love Boat*, or a golden statuette and a Golden Girl, or sushi and bait.

Television rarely inspires passion like a truly terrific film. Last night's *CSI* rerun is not nearly as likely to get you into a shouting match with your dad like an evening of *Brokeback Mountain* or *Desert Hearts*.

Also, with television you know that every seven minutes you're going to get a batch of obnoxious commercials. That means that every seven minutes you're getting more soda or checking your email. That is not the definition of being gripped by a story. Feel free to celebrate TV shows if you like, but for me the Primetime Emmy Awards are just not worthy of the festivities and party plans contained in this book.

That said, I do have to give some props to the Daytime Emmys. The soaps' kitsch factor is so high that this awards show rightfully boasts a small but ardent following. Those of us who keep TiVo-ing *The View* in case Barbara Walters clutches her boney chest and keels over in the middle of a "Why we hate thongs!" bitchfest have an understanding about this. Like a fetish for S&M, it's not for everyone, but there's definitely an appreciation for "good pain."

The Grammy® Awards?

The Grammys are OK, but hardly a party-inspiring event. Typically you only care about one or two genres of music, while the show presents, with equal bravura, everything from polka to rap to spoken word. If you're a pop fan, you could give a rat's ass about Best Classical Recording. If you're into rock, you're likely hate the country artists.

No, the only thing worthwhile about the Grammys

is the freak-show fashions. If the Oscars present *haute couture,* the Grammys give us a tits-to-the-wind parade of *faux pas* in fabric. As the saying goes, you can take the singer out of the trailer park…

And forget the jewelry. Don't expect to see Harry Winston loaning $500,000 diamond doodads to Kid freaking Rock. Queen Latifah, yes, but only at the Oscars. Call me a snob, but I believe a good rule of thumb is that when Van Cleef & Arpels declines to show, so do I.

The Tony Awards®?

If anything comes close to a really fun, classy show, it's the honoring of Broadway's best, the Tony Awards. This is the one awards ceremony put on with, by, and for people who have been thoroughly trained in how to behave in front of a live audience. They know how to be clever and charming, how to act gracious and humble, how to sing and dance and keep Debbie Allen away from the choreography. The trouble is, nobody cares because nobody goes to the theater.

I have to say, though, that part of the blame for the decline in theater attendance can be laid at the stage door. True, there's nothing like good live theater. Unfortunately, with producers regularly inserting *American Idol* castoffs into struggling musicals, there's often nothing like good live theater to be had. Plus, the sad fact is that Broadway is elitist. Who can afford to see all the shows, as wonderful as they sometimes are, at $125 a pop? And with Andrew Lloyd Webber still working, who would want to? Not only that, but it's only available in one place—New York—while every two-bit town in the country has *Mission: Impossible V—Tom Acts Normal* playing at the local mall. While thousands may go to Broadway shows every year, hundreds of *millions* go to the movies, and that's the shared experience necessary for a party-worthy awards show.

And the Winner Is…

Oscar. Plain and simple.

This book is to help you come up with a vision, and then create it—however large or small that may be. I'm not here to tell you that you *must* present a theme or dress up or serve these particular foods, or, indeed, do anything at all. Nor am I telling you that you have to purchase all the things discussed in this book. That goes for costumes, décor, prizes, gift goodies, everything, OK? *Pick and choose what works for you.* Although I'll warn you that once you get into it, your inner party monster just might come strutting out surprising you and everyone else!

Wait a minute. Prizes? Gift goodies? Costumes *and* décor? "What the hell," you may be asking yourself, "have I gotten myself into?"

Oh, honey!

You've gotten yourself into a fabulous and fun adventure in Academy Awards festivity. I am going to hold your moist little hand, even though I can just imagine where it has been, and lead you through everything it takes to throw the best damn Oscar party you and your friends have ever attended.

Spelled out in the ensuing chapters are many of the very same elements that go into the fabled *Vanity Fair* do, as well as Elton's party, the Governor's Ball, and the various studio parties. All the elaborate preparations these people spend hundreds of thousands of dollars creating for Hollywood's world-class glitterati have been scaled down to a level that even you—insignificant, unknown, drab little thing that you are—can make manifest in your own space. All you have to do is make some creative choices, purchase the items you desire, serve it up with panache, and host your own shindig.

—Joel Perry
August 2006

The Q Guide to
Oscar® Parties
and other award shows

QUIZ

Just How Much Do You Know About Oscar, Anyway?

1. Originally the statuette was made of bronze and plated with 24-karat gold. It stood on a base of black marble (except in 1945, when the pedestal was made slightly higher). Today, however, the Academy Award is made of britannium, a pewterlike alloy of copper, tin, and antimony. Because of other changes, what does the Oscar then get plated with today?

    a. Copper
    b. Nickel
    c. Silver
    d. Gold

2. How many inches does Oscar have?

    a. Eight and a half, on a warm day
    b. Ten, one for each of the studio heads (Paramount: 1; Metro + Goldwyn + Mayer = 3; Warner Bros.: 3; 20th

Century Fox: 1; RKO (Radio-Keith-Orpheum): 2; Total: 10)

c. *Twelve, but we don't like to brag*

d. *Thirteen and a half. Slightly less when emerging from the ocean*

3. How heavy is Oscar?

    a. *Eight and a half pounds (equal to the amount of sincerity in Hollywood)*

    b. *Ten pounds even (power-walking with one in each hand is excellent cardio)*

    c. *Eleven and a half pounds (only slightly more than an Olsen twin)*

    d. *Heavy enough to get an interview with Barbara Walters—and that's all that matters*

4. Created by MGM art director Cedric Gibbons in 1927, the design depicts a knight holding a crusader's sword, standing on a reel of film with five spokes. What do those spokes represent?

    a. *The number of times you have to be nominated before you can win*

    b. *The average number of producers you have to sleep with to get a part*

    c. *The original branches of the Academy:*

actors, writers, directors, producers, and technicians

d. *The original studios that founded the Academy in order to promote their films: Paramount, MGM, Warner Bros., 20th Century Fox, and RKO*

5. Originally sculpted in 1927 by out-of-work sculptor George Stanley for $500, Oscar's official name is:

   a. *The Academy Award for Film Excellence*
   b. *The Academy Award of Merit*
   c. *The Academy Award of Distinction*
   d. *The Thing Dreams Are Made Of*

6. The Academy did not adopt the name "Oscar" until 1939. So how did this award come to be called that?

   a. *Margaret Herrick, who was the Academy librarian (later to become its executive director!), said it came from when she first saw it and exclaimed, "It looks like my Uncle Oscar!"*
   b. *When Bette Davis won an award, she claimed to comment that it looked like her husband, Harmon Oscar Nelson. Supposedly, others who overheard her*

passed on the nickname.

c. Hollywood entertainment reporter Sidney Skolsky used the name to describe the statuette Katharine Hepburn won for Morning Glory *(1932–1933). He said he chose that name to "negate pretension." As if someone named Oscar couldn't have a diva's ego!*

Other Fun Facts:

- Basic value: $330.
- For three years during World War II, they were made of painted plaster. After the war, recipients were able to trade those in for metal ones.
- Since 1983, R. S. Owens & Co. of Chicago has been retained to make the award.
- Since 2000, when a shipment of 55 of that year's Oscars were stolen off a loading dock in Bell, California (53 were later recovered next to a dumpster in LA's Koreatown), the Academy keeps an entire show's worth handy so as not to get caught with their tux pants down again.

CHAPTER ONE

Deciding on a Theme and Making It Happen

"I would rather be here with you than anywhere else in the world."

—Faye Dunaway as Joan Crawford in *Mommie Dearest* (1981) addressing the fans and press in front of her house after hearing on the radio that she won the Oscar

OTHER THAN your fabulous self, the first thing that will greet your guests upon arrival is the environment. Let's hope that's at least a clean house, although if it truly looks like hell you can claim your theme is *Twister* or *Seven*. But the environment is a blank canvas upon which you can paint the theme for your party. If there's nothing going on with it, (a) you missed a prime opportunity to impress, and (b) you might as well be straight. I mean, homosexuals are known for our ability to invent and have serious fun. This is your chance to sparkle, doll face. Grab it and indulge! God knows there's little enough else out there that's half as festive. OK, there's Gay Pride, but until the weather heats up and shirts come off, I'm just saying don't let the Oscars go by without really going for the all-out event at least once. And that involves selecting a theme and decorating. Then run, Forrest, run with that theme!

Naturally the subject of movies is a fertile field, but there are so many to choose from that it can be daunting. If you have a flat-out favorite flick of all time, that's the one. You'll have the passion to do what it takes to bring it to life and share it with your friends. Plus, it will make your shindig that much more fun for you as host.

If you still need help, well, darling, I'm here to give you suggestions. Start by looking at the films that were big this year because they're the ones the majority of your guests will likely have seen. That familiarity will add to their appreciation of your festivities. If the nominations have already come out, consult that list. Do any of those titles get your creative bodily fluids moving? If so, go with the flow. After all, this is supposed to be fun, right? Of course, right!

Choosing Among Many

"I'd like the coffin to be white, and I want it specially lined with satin. White...or pink. Maybe red! Bright, flaming red! Let's make it gay!"

—Gloria Swanson as Norma Desmond, who thinks Joe is a funeral director in *Sunset Boulevard* (1950)

Perhaps there are two or more movies that intrigue you. How do decide between them? No problem. Ask yourself which would be the easiest and most effective to go with. Say you're torn between three choices: One is a searing *American Beauty*–type of family drama; another is based on a graphic novel set in the 1920s with a *Dick Tracy* look; and the third is a Japanese costume drama along the lines of *Memoirs of a Geisha*. Since you want to avoid the tragedy of plunging into something you're not going to be able to pull off, let's examine these three choices for practicality:

1. While a Japanese costume drama can certainly be worked into a theme, it's a hell of a lot of work. Do you have the time, willingness, and resources to make it happen? If so, you totally rule—so go for it if that's what gets you off. But for most of us, that likelihood ain't so great.

2. The clothes and props for the family drama are going to look an awful lot like the stuff most people already have. That's going to make it tough to present as a noticeable theme for your party. I recommend passing.

3. With a fedora and a trench coat, you're well on your way to the 1920s with enough money left over to redo your Oscar-viewing space in twenties noir, plus get some decent eats and alcohol. This theme will be the easiest and most effective to recreate in your humble abode.

Other Theme Ideas

If this year's movies aren't turning your crank, there are plenty of great Oscar and non-Oscar films for the past to consider. Below are some possibilities. Go with one of them or use this list to inspire you to greater and better things.

Themes

Movies with definite "looks" that you can easily interpret for your party:

Planet of the Apes

Star Wars

Horror (avoid monster flicks, that's *so* Halloween)
To Wong Foo..., Priscilla: Queen of the Desert, etc.
Westerns
Chicago
Samurai
Harry Potter and the Fabulous Oscar Party
Sunset Boulevard
The Three Musketeers
Take your pick of military movies from *M*A*S*H*
    to *Top Gun*
American Graffiti
Kung fu flicks
Tarzan films (who cares that they never won Oscars,
    it's all about the loincloths!)
Lawrence of Arabia
Bible movies (think lots and lots of fabric)
Valley of the Dolls
Classic Disney cartoons
Titanic
James Bond (take your pick of the Bonds)
Pirates of the Caribbean (a personal favorite—pirates
    show skin and don't shave)
A Great Big Hollywood Awards Show (duh!)

Cliché but popular

Moulin Rouge (because everyone thinks they're either
    Nicole or Ewan)
Lord of the Rings (a D&D nerd's wet dream)
Clockwork Orange (an excuse to experiment with
    false eyelashes)
The Wizard of Oz (like you don't already have the
    slippers)

Gone With the Wind (maybe Rhett will carry *you* up
the stairs)

The Sound of Music (lederhosen for everyone!)

Saturday Night Fever (love those tight-crotch/
exposed-bust '70s)

One Million Years B.C. (guarantees lots of sexy
bare skin)

Note of Caution

Settle on *one* theme. If you're torn between two, do one
this year and the other next. Mixing and matching doesn't
work, so don't even try. I had a friend who did that and
it never worked: Guests became utterly confused when
his announced theme was, say, *Rain Man of La Mancha*
or *Gangs of New York, New York*. I mean, what do you
wear when the theme is *The Zorro and the Pity*? Go with
a single theme, OK?

Four Bargain-Basement Theme Alternatives

PARTY STORE, PART 1: Go to the party store the day after
Christmas. (Yes, you'll have to plan for it, so go easy
on the eggnog.) When you get there, all things Christmas will be at rock-bottom prices. Snap 'em up! Why?
Because there are dozens of movies that have a Christmas theme: *White Christmas, A Christmas Story, The Ref,
Christmas With the Kranks, I'll Be Home for Christmas,
Miracle on 34th Street, Bad Santa, It's a Wonderful Freaking Life*—the list goes on and on. But you can only get
away with this once. Do it twice and people will know
exactly what you've been up to.

PARTY STORE, PART 2: OK, you didn't get there in time for the Christmas loot. Go to the party store anyway, see what they have for 75 percent off, and buy it *all*. Be the first on your block to host a *SpongeBob SquarePants* Oscar party. Or Pooh, or Barbie, or Power Rangers, or whatever the hell they're trying to unload that week. Really and truly get into whatever you bought. Talk like SpongeBob—"This is the best awards *ever!*" Dress like Barbie or Ken. Jump around like a Power Ranger (and try to remember that not everyone can be the pink one). If you play it up big, nobody will know you bought the cheap shit; they'll think you're zany and borderline brilliant. Own it! Go with the cheese!

TRAILER-TRASH PARTY: Gather mismatched chairs, preferably those folding-aluminum grandpa-sitting-in-the-yard-hanging-out-of-his-boxers chairs. Move your nice furniture out and this crap in. Artfully scatter crushed empty beer cans (the cheap-ass brands) thither and yon. Dress in cut-off jeans and a filthy wife-beater, or pull out your Daisy Dukes. Catering is beans and franks, Cheetos, pork rinds, and pickled eggs. Ringworm adds an authentic touch.

MINIMALISM: This requires that you buy absolutely nothing, so I know you're already crushing on this idea. But it is work. Move all of your furniture out of the party area (except the television). Take everything off the walls—photos, art, mirrors, curtains, everything—and store it where it will not be seen. You may need to scrub where your wall hangings left those dirty shadow marks, because the idea is a very clean look: a completely empty space with utterly blank walls. Set the television on the floor in the center of the room. That lone single piece will emphasize the emptiness of the room and give you the starkness this look requires. Guests sit on the floor because, damn it, that's where minimalists sit! Dress simply, wearing either all white or all black. Shave your head.

The thing to remember is this: If you think doing any of these is lame, you're right. Your attitude about it will be evident to your guests, and they'll be embarrassed because you're embarrassed. However...if you think this is genius, *you will also be right*. Your guests will pick up on the sheer wacky fun as reflected in your ballsy attitude toward it. So embrace the silliness! Celebrate the insanity! Commit to the kitsch!

That's what makes any theme work!

Making the Décor Happen

Congratulations, you've selected a theme. Now it's time to make your party environment reflect that theme.

If you selected a particular movie, see it again. As you watch it, keep a list of prominent props, costumes, and scenery. This might be difficult if the movie is still only in theaters and you're doing this in the dark, but try. If anyone gives you looks, just say, "Film student." In New York or LA, that'll be the end of it. But if you're a "film student" in Lubbock, Texas, or Ypsilanti, Michigan, that's so sad they might even give you a dollar. Put it toward your décor.

Once you've created that list, look it over in a nice

relaxing place like your home or Starbucks or while getting your pedicure.

- Put a happy face next to the items you already have.
- Put an asterisk next to the items you know you can borrow from others.
- Put an ugly old dollar sign next to the items you're going to have to spring for.

Here's an example of what such a list might look like:

My Big-Ass Oscar Party Needs

☺ Chairs

✳ TV—ask Tom and Bill, see if they know how to steal cable, too

✳ Floor Pillows—ask Ted, Marianne, Scott

$ Paper plates/plastic cups—I am so not doing dishes!

$ Prizes—DVDs (Note: Make list and see what's on sale/bargain bin.) [Note: Prizes and swag-bag items are covered in Chapter Five.]

✳ Sling—ask Mistress Darkness, can we convert hers to a *Moulin Rouge*–type swing?

☺ Fabric

☺ Bedazzler

✳ Lighting—Prof. Rose at Community Collage, remind him I sat his kids during last fall's *'Night Mother.*

$ Swag bags—movie candy, tchotchkes, samples, copies of this book

☺ Cinco de Mayo napkins and chips (Query:

Will people notice chips are from last year, too?)

$ Bartenders—because bitch Robert won't. Would Patty do it cheap?

$ Other help? (Possible: catering, cleanup, serving, etc.)

☺ Talent and flawless skin

☺ Flowers—technically next door, but late at night who'll know?

$ Strippers? Too much? Maybe if Jill gets drunk enough she'll do?

$ Booze! (Check to see what I can steal from Mom first.)

$ Food

Now then, use this list to organize everything into three dedicated lists. Start with three more sheets of paper. On the first one write "I Have" at the top. Under that write down everything on your list that had a smiley face (☺) beside it. On the second sheet write "Must Borrow" at the top and then all the items that you placed an asterisk (*) by. And on the third sheet do the same, heading it "Must Buy" and listing the stuff you had dollar signs by ($). Now let's take a look at each.

That Which You Have

For the things you already have, make sure you really do have them—and your loving domestic partner didn't throw them out with go-go boots. Assemble what you can in one place. Obviously if one of the items is the upstairs day bed that you intend to strip so you can create that perfect *Kiss of the Spider Woman* jail cell, you can leave that where it is until the day of the event. But all the rest gather up in a big box, or create a space where it will not be disturbed. That way you'll know where your selected items are and can move on to other things.

That Which You Borrow

For the items you will need to borrow, start making your phone calls now. Keep in mind that it probably means you'll have to invite them, so weigh that before contacting them. This is an excellent opportunity to reconnect with old friends and exes. Once you've caught up on their new jobs, lovers, and STDs, you can casually ask if you may borrow that item you're lusting after for your party. "So, Ted," you may say, "do you still have that giant cross left over from the *Fashion of the Christ* Pride Parade float that upset the fundies so much the year Mel's Christian snuff film came out?"

The best idea is to enroll them in helping you. Keep in mind "enroll" is not "enlist." You're not *telling* them to help you, you're *asking*. Get your friend excited about what you're doing and dangle the possibility of letting them be a part of the fun you're creating. Be nice. Smile. Work the compliments. (You know how to lie; you do it all the time online.) If none of this worked, feel free to resort to offers of cash and/or sex. Just get the damn item!

Once the details have been arranged, *go collect it before they change their mind.* If it's bulky, make arrangements to pick it up. Again, the sooner the better. If they change their mind, it'll be harder for them to take it back if it's on your property.

That Which You Must Shell Out For

Now it's time to look at those items you marked with dollar signs. First of all, now that you've assembled the stuff you had hanging around the house and have a good idea of what you can borrow, do you really need to go buying stuff? There are budget considerations, and you want to make sure you have some moolah left over for (a) your fabulous outfit, (b) party prizes and swag, and (c) booze. Or at least refreshments.

Still feel you simply *must* have that captain's wheel for your *Titanic*-themed party? (And must it be tired old *Titanic*? Can't you affix it to the ceiling for a *Poseidon* feel?) Well, before you waltz into a nautical supply store and purchase it outright, consider if you're ever going to use the damn thing again. If not, that's going to be one hell of an expensive lawn ornament. So here's the tip: Whether it's antiques or wall hangings or other specialty items, *see if you can't rent it first.*

Lying Your Way to Free Décor

Tell whoever's in charge that you need it as a prop for a benefit party. Never mind that the benefit is *you*. If you can come up with a decent story, they might even loan it free. Try "I'm throwing a fundraiser for the [your town] underprivileged who need treatment they cannot get locally." Which is not entirely a lie. You and your guests are "underprivileged" because on Oscar night you will all be in *your* house and not in the Kodak Theater in Hollywood, and the "treatment" you need but cannot get locally is Star Treatment.

By the way, if the idea of actually throwing an honest-to-god benefit party appeals to you, then you and your favorite charity are in luck! I cover that in Chapter Two.

If a bald-faced lie makes you uncomfortable, try a smaller one. After all, if you sell the store owner on a charity benefit for the needy, he or she may get all enthusiastic and want to attend. Do you really want uninitiated straight people struggling to cope with your *Pink Flamingos*–themed party when you pass around the unwrapped Tootsie Rolls? To prevent having to explain the joke (and why guests keep licking the furniture), simply tell a different little fib like, oh, that you're a photographer and you need the item(s) for a shoot. Come on, you do intend to take pictures, right? Let it drop that you're a photography *student* (translation: poor), and you might even sucker them into letting you use it for free. Arrange to pick up the stuff on the Friday afternoon before your "shoot." Naturally you'll want to return it at the first opportunity—and in pristine condition, too, so keep 'em away from the action if your theme is *Mad Max: Beyond Thunderdome*. After all, your Oscar party is going to be so wonderful and talked about that you'll want to do this all again next year, so don't burn any bridges by returning beatup stuff. Also, if something does get trashed, be prepared to make full and immediate compensation. That's what you get for jumping up on a rented card table to shout "I'm king of the world!"

Q List #1:
Money, Money, Money!

Did you ever wonder just what keeps the Academy afloat? ABC pays about $20 mil a year for the broadcast rights to the Academy Awards ceremony. That's a lot of money and it pretty much bankrolls the entire annual operating budget of the Academy.

Things $20 million would buy:

- Bruce Willis in a lead role
- 172 H2 Hummer SUTs
- 50,000 60 GB iPods
- 338,983 adult day passes to Disneyland, or one for each person in Anchorage, Alaska
- 23,255,813 condoms
- 178,904 "Decadent Indulgence Vibrators" from SpicyGear.com (with batteries and shipping, of course, otherwise what's the point?)
- 667,111 copies of the Indigo Girls' box set, including "Indigo Girls," "Strange Fire," and "Nomads, Indians, Saints"
- 500,000 bottles of Taittinger Brut La Française champagne
- 1,544,401 copies of this book (at $12.95). Enough for all the people in Philadelphia queer or straight!—plus over 75,000 left over for their swag bags!

Breaking Down and Spending Some Dough

Every city of moderate size has places that rent things. Check in your Yellow Pages and drop by to check 'em out. If you're looking for fairly standard items, they may have what you need. Don't forget specialty rental stores, either. A medical supply house could outfit you very nicely for a *One Flew Over the Cuckoo's Nest* party.

Army surplus stores are one-stop shopping for just about any relatively modern military movie: *Platoon*, *Deer Hunter*, *Apocalypse Now*, *Patton*. Anything prior to World War II is probably going to be problematic, so don't expect to get your *Glory* outfits here. And since this is the *U.S.* Army Surplus, you can forget anything *Das Boot,* too.

And finally, don't skip over party stores. Larger ones will have all kinds of party-theme crap at affordable prices. True, their themes are not going to be for specific movies, but you can take what they have and *call* it something else. For instance, those tiki torches, grass skirts, and other cheesy luau items could be décor for *South Pacific*, *Hawaii*, *Blue Hawaii*, or, for you Dick Van Dyke/Nancy Kwan fans, *Lt. Robin Crusoe, U.S.N.* Since straight people are allowed to get married anytime—not that I'm bitter about that or anything—party stores always have wedding stuff out the ass. Think *Muriel's Wedding*, *The Wedding Crashers*, *My Big Fat Greek Wedding*, or *Scenes from a Marriage*. Well, maybe not that last one. Oh, and there's always Happy Birthday decorations if you're perverse and want *The Boys in the Band* as your theme. Just don't expect a crowd the following year.

If there remain items you still need to purchase for your party, so be it. Go forth, open your wallet, and aid the economy. Buy what you need, but unless you're David Geffen, *keep the receipt*, darling, and take it all back on Monday. Just because you're watching Hollywood millionaires on TV doesn't make you one.

CHAPTER TWO

The Benefit Party

"My peers say I have made a difference. That means more to me than winning an Oscar."

—Ten-time Oscar nominee for Best Cinematography and three-time winner, Conrad Hall

BIG PROPS to you! You have generously decided to make a difference and use the frivolity and festivity of the Oscars (or whichever other awards show, see Chapter Eleven) to benefit somebody other than yourself. How mature, how community minded, how sexylicious does that make you? Answer: A lot.

So let's get started, shall we?

There are three main differences between a private just-for-giggles get-together and your benefit party that will be collecting funds to help the world and all who live in it. Other than these differences, your party runs the same as described in the other chapters. But these differences need to be observed.

Big Difference #1

You must tell your guests it's a benefit party when you invite them. If they arrive expecting a regular party, and you hit them up for money, they are rightfully going to be angry and take it out on your reputation, breakables, linens, and unsecured jewelry. I cannot stress this enough—your guests *must* know that this is a fundraiser. So make that explicitly clear every step of the way:

1. When you invite them.
2. Every time you talk to them about it later over the phone or brunch.
3. When you greet them at the door.

This does two things. First, it lets your guests know that a pitch for money is coming so that when they arrive they are not caught off-guard. Second, since they know it's a benefit, they'll bring their checkbooks. Why? Because you told them to when you told them it was a benefit! And you remind them when they arrive so they know there's no chance of getting out of being expected to cough up some dough.

Don't be shy about telling people you're hosting a benefit. We all love to feel good about ourselves and donating to worthy causes gives the check writer that warm and fuzzy glow. Remember, you're creating a fun-filled opportunity for your guests to make the world a better place. Don't worry about it; they'll understand that, and they'll be fine with it. And you will be a hero for directing generous donations to organizations that help others.

Let me show you how easy it is with a couple of examples. First, the written invite (with explanatory notes) useful for printed invitations or for the online e-invite:

You are cordially invited to
Pat Smith's Oscar Party [a]

Benefiting [your charity of choice] [b]
[brief description of what it does here] [c]

Date: Sunday, February 27, 2008
Time: 4:00 pm until ???
Address: 1234 Homo Lane, Queerville,
USA 69069

Dress: Whatever fits a Titanic theme—
from first class to steerage—but don't set
sail without your checkbook! [d]

Checks can be made out to [charity]. [e]

---

a) tells people the reason for your party as well as the brilliant person throwing it.
b) tells your guests right up front that this is a fundraising party, and which organization is going to benefit.
c) tells what your chosen charity does, thereby

educating them and making them feel
comfortable about donating to it.

d) tells people you are fun—"Oh, look at that,
a theme! I'm going to have so much fun
I won't care about forking over my hard-
earned money"—and reminds them once
again to bring the checkbook.

e) reminds them one last time that they'll be
writing a check, and gives them the option
of having it written and ready when they get
there.

By the way, the e-invite websites are very useful. You
can check back on the site at any time to see who has
responded yes and who's passing on your party with a big,
stupid no and lame excuse. This makes it easy to keep a
running tally of who's coming instead of your having to
maintain a list of the people who called or wrote back.

. . .

Then there's the telephone or word-of-mouth invitation:

"Hey, Chris! This is Casey. I'm calling to invite you
to my no-holds-barred, full-on Oscar party, because it
couldn't happen without you, you crazy whore! [a] Get this,
though, we're not only gonna get smashed and trash the
Oscars, but it's gonna be for a great cause! It's a benefit
party for [your charity of choice [b]], could you die? They're
those people who [brief description of what they do [c]],
and we *love* them for that. So bring your checkbook [d] and
your loincloth because it's a totally *Tarzan* theme. Swear
to God. I'm having banana daiquiris and gift bags so don't

you dare miss it, OK?[e] It's at [time and place] and I'm counting on you to win at least one of the competitions so we can crown you—or whoever wins—king and/or queen of the jungle![f] Oops, the cat's on fire, gotta go! Buh-bye!"

a) tells your guest how special you think they are. (they won't know you used the same script on all 150 invitees.)

b) tells your guests right up front that this is a fundraising party, and which organization is going to benefit from the donations.

c) tells what your chosen charity does, thereby educating them and making them feel comfortable about donating to it.

d) reminds them again that they're going to be writing a check.

e) tells people what fun you have planned, thereby making the giving up of cash a pain-less thing. It also informs them of the theme and how you expect them to dress—or, in this case, not dress.

f) Competitions? How exciting! This party is so totally going to be worth it!

Big Difference #2

You should *contact the charity you intend to collect funds for*. There are several reasons for this:

- You need to know they haven't gone out of business. (Hey, it happens. And how embar-rassing would that be?)

- You need to know where to deliver the fund-age you collect.
- If they have a local representative, they may be willing to send someone over to your party to make a five-minute pitch for the charity to maximize giving. (Yes, they get to stay for the whole party. What kind of host are you?)
- They may have a video or DVD that makes the pitch for you.
- If a rep can't come and you are going to be making the pitch yourself, they can guide you as to what to say, give you talking points, or send you information that will help you do this.
- There are tax rules about donations and what is acceptable as a receipt that vary from state to state. Your charity will be able to advise you on this. That way, you'll know what to tell Rosie O'Donnell when she donates you $100,000.
- They may be able to provide you with the names of some establishments or business owners who are big supporters of their cause. (More about this later.)

Big Difference #3

This will help you raise awareness of your charity and, more important, give you some fab options for your swag bags. Remember asking your charity for the names of business owners that supported their cause? Oh, please, it was in the list about four inches above and

I know you know what four inches looks like. OK, then. You asked them for that information so you could hit up these businesses for whatever gifties they may be able to give you for your swag bags!

Tell the owner-slash-manager you're holding a benefit party for _____, their favorite charity. You invite them (and a guest). Then you ask if they have any samples or coupons for services you could put in the swag bags you'll be giving your guests. It's a great way for the business to reach out to new customers, and you get to have interesting and varied stuff for your bags. How cool is that?

After you've gone to all the "leads" provided by the charity, it's time to turn to friends, clients, and others. Basically you tell them the same thing and try to charm them, too, into donating goods, samples, or services, In case you need help with this, it's covered in more depth in Chapter Five.

Make a list of who gave you which swag-bag goodies, so you remember whom to thank them afterward—and whom to hit up again for next year's party!

When Do You Collect the Cash?

I recommend doing it just before the Oscar telecast begins. That way, it's done and everyone can forget about it and concentrate on enjoying the show and your party.

The pitch can be earlier, say, an hour beforehand. At that time announce—loudly and explicitly in a perky voice—that you will be collecting everyone's generous donations just before the Oscar show. That allows time for people to write their checks and for you to talk it up among your guests. It also lets people know that it's coming and there's no way out.

As the pre-show winds down on TV, remind everyone to get their checks ready because you'll be collecting as soon as it ends. The instant it does, *seize that moment!* Announce that it's collection time and pass among your guests with a hat or other receptacle. You can have a minion or two assist. Let people know you want it *now*— because the show is about to start! Do it right and your collection of the cash will become part of the excitement of the Oscar show itself!

Once collected, store the checks and money in a secure location. During the commercial breaks before they give out the Best Director, Actor, Actress, and Picture awards, pass the hat again to make sure you get money from any latecomers. After the party get it to your intended charity.

Which Charity Will You Choose?

There's a glorious pile of legitimate and worthy charities out there. All you have to do is select one and run with it. Or to it. Every community has local charities, and the sheer number makes it impossible to present any kind of comprehensive list in this book. Here are some of the most common:

- Local institutions serving your area
- Educational programs
- Organizations that raise money to help fight specific diseases
- Bike rides or walks for AIDS, cancer, Alzheimer's, etc.

- A political party (or an apolitical party)
- Organizations that help with homelessness or feeding the needy
- Domestic-abuse shelters
- Law-enforcement charities
- Legal aid
- Organizations that support the arts
- Ecological concerns
- Churches and temples with affirming congregations
- Animal charities
- The Sisters of Perpetual Indulgence (www.thesisters.org)
- Whatever the hell *you* feel like supporting!

Candy kisses for Prizes

Q List #2:
The Most Oscars

Top 10 Films (plus four more) with the Most Oscars Won

(The only one of these that did not win Best Picture is *Cabaret*. And speaking of musicals, for you musical-theater queens, I would point out that four of these, or 28.6% were musicals, thank you!)

Ben Hur (1951) with 11
Titanic (1997) with 11
The Lord of the Rings: The Return of the King (2003) with 11

West Side Story (1961) with 10

Gigi (1958) with 9

The Last Emperor (1987) with 9

The English Patient (1996) with 9

Gone With the Wind (1939) with 8

From Here to Eternity (1953) with 8

On the Waterfront (1954) with 8

My Fair Lady (1964) with 8

Cabaret (1972) with 8

Gandhi (1982) with 8

Amadeus (1984) with 8

Top 10 Most Nominated Films

TOP TIER

All About Eve (1950) with 14

Titanic (1997) with 14

SECOND TIER

Gone With the Wind (1939) with 13

From Here to Eternity (1953) with 13

Mary Poppins (1964) with 13

Who's Afraid of Virginia Woolf? (1966) with 13

Forrest Gump (1994) with 13

Shakespeare in Love (1998) with 13

The Lord of the Rings: Fellowship of the Ring (2001) with 13

Chicago (2002) with 13

Most Oscars for Best Actor

(In alphabetical order; each has two)

Marlon Brando: *On the Waterfront* (1954) and *The Godfather* (1972—refused)

Gary Cooper: *Sergeant York* (1941) and

High Noon (1952)

Tom Hanks: *Philadelphia* (1993) and *Forrest Gump* (1994)

Dustin Hoffman: *Kramer vs. Kramer* (1979) and *Rain Man* (1988)

Fredric March: *Dr. Jekyll and Mr. Hyde* (1931–32) and *The Best Years of Our Lives* (1946)

Jack Nicholson: *One Flew Over the Cuckoo's Nest* (1975) and *As Good as It Gets* (1997)

Spencer Tracy: *Captains Courageous* (1937) and *Boys Town* (1938)

Most Oscars for Best Supporting Actor:

Walter Brennan with three: *Come and Get It* (1936), *Kentucky* (1938), and *The Westerner* (1940)

Actor with Most Oscars:

(A TIE, THREE EACH)

Walter Brennan: *Come and Get It* (1936), *Kentucky* (1938), and *The Westerner* (1940)—all as Best Supporting Actor

Jack Nicholson: *One Flew Over the Cuckoo's Nest* (1975) and *As Good as It Gets* (1997)—both as Best Actor; plus *Terms of Endearment* (1983)—as Best Supporting Actor

Most Oscars for Best Actress:

Katharine Hepburn with four: *Morning Glory* (1932–33), *Guess Who's Coming to Dinner?* (1967), *The Lion in Winter* (1968), and *On Golden Pond* (1981)

Most Oscars for Best Supporting Actress:

(A TIE, TWO EACH)

Dianne Wiest: *Hannah and Her Sisters* (1986) and *Bullets Over Broadway* (1994)

Shelley Winters: *The Diary of Anne Frank* (1959) and *A Patch of Blue* (1965)

Actress with Most Oscars:

Katharine Hepburn with four: *Morning Glory* (1932–33), *Guess Who's Coming to Dinner?* (1967), *The Lion in Winter* (1968), and *On Golden Pond* (1981)—all Best Actress

Coming in second is Ingrid Bergman with three: *Gaslight* (1934) and *Anastasia* (1956) —both as Best Actress; plus *Murder on the Orient Express* (1974)—as Best Supporting Actress

Most Oscars for Best Director:

John Ford with four: *The Informer* (1935), *The Grapes of Wrath* (1940), *How Green Was My Valley* (1941), and *The Quiet Man* (1952)

COMING IN SECOND IS A TIE, WITH THREE APIECE:

William Wyler: *Mrs. Miniver* (1942), *The Best Years of Our Lives* (1946), and *Ben Hur* (1959)

Frank Capra: *It Happened One Night* (1934), *Mr. Deeds Goes to Town* (1936), and *You Can't Take It With You* (1938)

CHAPTER THREE

Appropriate Apparel

QUOTE

"As you can see, I did receive my Academy booklet on how to dress like a serious actress."

—Cher, presenting in her fabulous Bob Mackie black-Mohawk-witch dress the 58th Annual Academy Awards after being snubbed for *Mask* (1985)

EVEN BEFORE your guests arrive at your swell soiree, they will face the issue of selecting just what to wear. By informing them of your chosen theme, you will give them clear guidance.

However you invite your guests, make sure you tell them what theme (if any) they will encounter. Notify them far enough in advance that they have time to assemble the necessary clothes. For instance, a *Beach Blanket Bingo* theme is simple because it signals board shorts and a tanning session, while the demands of a *Dangerous Liaisons* or *Camelot* theme will take longer and involve more arduous preparation. (If you slyly chose a beachy theme to get your guests to show lots of skin, be kind enough to compensate by turning up the heat in the room accordingly. This *is* winter, people.)

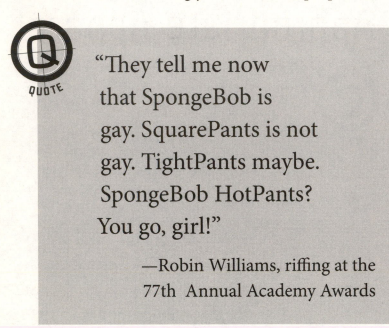

"They tell me now that SpongeBob is gay. SquarePants is not gay. TightPants maybe. SpongeBob HotPants? You go, girl!"

—Robin Williams, riffing at the 77th Annual Academy Awards

The Host's *Ensemble*

It is you, my dear one, who sets the tone of the party. Guests arrive with all sorts of possibilities in their head of what may or may not happen, as well as ideas as to what kind of behavior they should—or could—indulge in. It is the host who gives them the cues for what the evening holds.

For instance, if you open the door in a James Bond tuxedo holding a martini, your guests can expect an urbane evening of 007 silliness and, if you're a lesbian, archly male drag. If, on the other hand, you greet your guests wearing a *Showgirls* g-string, you are creating an entirely different set of expectations and had better have the enthusiasm to follow through later. Don't get me wrong, I'm not at all against that kind of party. But don't be surprised if you find yourself distracted by the pole dancing when you're trying to tally Oscar ballots.

Your guests will look to you both to set the boundaries and to pique their excitement. The way you choose to present yourself through the clothes you wear, your demeanor, and your degree of drunkenness will set the initial tone of the evening.

So what you present to your guests on all levels is important. What you wear doesn't have to be an actual costume, but I encourage you to consider assembling, borrowing, renting, or appropriating one. Costumes always add a festive quality, and what's the point of any party if we're not pumping up the festive quotient? If you can't be bothered to create a look for yourself, at least augment your Dockers and polo shirt with something that says "fun." To do that, you'll need to know the difference between "fun" and just plain tragic.

Items That Shout "Fun"!

Feather boa

Tux jacket

Sequins! And there's no such thing as "too many"!

Top hat (if it has to be paper, so be it)

Long strands of pearls

Wig—the bigger and higher the better

Heels!—ditto

Items That Say "Sad"

- Easter bunny outfit
- Santa suit
- Ghost (sheet) costume
- Any tired outfit from another holiday
- Culottes
- Clothes from Sears

Give Yourself Time to Prepare!

QUOTE

"Why do they have these things so early? I mean, no woman can look good at five o' clock in the afternoon. Except, possibly, Tatum O'Neal."

—Maggie Smith as actress Diana Barrie complaining about the Oscar ceremony in *California Suite* (1978)

A final word about dressing for your party: Allow yourself ample time to do what it takes to make yourself presentable. If that's a beauty regimen that begins 48 hours prior, plan for it. If it only takes you 15 minutes to throw on what you're going to wear and do the requisite fluff and puff, that's great, just make sure you've given yourself that time.

If you don't, you'll be a nervous wreck and sweating like a pig, and that's no way to begin Oscar night. What, you think Shirley MacLaine is yanking up her L'eggs control tops in the limo? No, no, no. She is all set to go and centering herself by breathing and trying to forget *Bewitched*. You should be doing the same thing. So forgo the drama of an insane last-minute rush by doing the following:

1. Know how long it's going to take you to get pretty. (For demonstration purposes let's say that is one hour.)
2. Give yourself another half hour so you'll have a comfortable cushion of time in case something goes wrong.
3. Add those together: 1 hour + ½ hour = 1½ hours.
4. Subtract that amount of time from the start of your party. If your Oscar party begins at 7:00 p.m. (we're talking East Coast here), that means you count backward 1½ hours from 7:00, which is 5:30.
5. Set an alarm or buzzer for that time, so you won't forget.
6. Also write that time down on a large piece of paper and post it where you will see it as you prepare for your party that day. That will help you keep it in mind so that time won't sneak up on you and be a surprise when the alarm or buzzer you set goes off.

7. When the alarm rings, *stop whatever you are doing* and start getting *yourself* ready! If every single little preparation hasn't quite gotten done yet, *let it go!* (We'll address those issues in another chapter.)

8. When you are dressed and ready, *relax*. Do not go back to party prep. It will make you crazy and sweaty, and unless you are Angelina Jolie in *Girl, Interrupted*, that is not going to work for you.

Ahhh! See? You are cool, calm, and collected. In control. And most important, you look *maaah-velous!* You are refreshed and ready to regale your guests with the best damn Oscar party they have ever attended.

Youngest and Oldest

"Welcome to the 75th Annual Academy Awards ceremony. Oh, I wish I could be 75 years old again."

—Kirk Douglas at age 86, copresenting the Best Picture award

If you thought being seen as old or young mattered at the bar, that's nothing compared to how it goes down in Hollywood. So to celebrate those actors and actresses who are, as they say, "of a certain age," we present this short quiz in their honor. Don't spend too much time on it. Remember, the clock is ticking and you're getting older every second.

1. Who is the youngest Oscar winner?

2. Who is the oldest Best Actor winner?

3. Who is the oldest Best Supporting Actor winner? (No, it's not Kirk.)

Youngest and Oldest

4. Who is the oldest Best Actress winner?

5. Who is the oldest actor ever to receive an Oscar?

6. Who is the oldest actress ever to receive an Oscar?

CHAPTER FOUR

Food and Drink

"Aragorn, let's find some food."

—John Rhys-Davies as Gimli in
*Lord of the Rings: The Return
of the King* (2003)

ON THE most basic level, as long as you have something your guests can cram in their pie-holes while watching the TV and shouting, "Why can't you adopt *me!*" at Angelina Jolie, you'll be fine. On the other hand, your guests could expect that kind of food at any crappy Oscar party in town. Is that what you want?

I know, I know, being gay means there's a certain pressure to provide that little something extra that we don't always feel motivated to produce. You know, crudités that go beyond carrots and celery to include white asparagus and purple Hawaiian sweet potatoes. Who could blame you if you didn't feel like getting on board with that b.s.

However . . . this is an Academy Awards party. This is your time to shine. And you're not doing it just by yourself. You have Oscar. And me.

So let's buckle down and look at your theme. It only takes a little imagination to match your theme to a movie, and you'll be off and concocting your own cuisine in no time. Here's a list that demonstrates what you could do.

Planet of the Apes: bananas everything—daiquiris, pudding, Foster, you name it

Star Wars: regular fare with food dye to look otherworldly

Horror: regular food chopped up and dyed red for blood and gray for mold

To Wong Foo..., Priscilla: Queen of the Desert, etc.: salads (a girl has to watch her weight)

Westerns: ribs, beans, Jake Gyllenhaal

Chicago: prison food, bathtub gin

Samurai: sushi, Japanese take-out

Harry Potter and the Fabulous Oscar Party: regular food, just call it "bat burgers" and "wizard's wine"

Sunset Boulevard: how about satay, just call it "dead monkey meat"?

The Three Musketeers: fire-roasted chicken served on swords

Military movies: MREs (Meals Ready to Eat) from Army Surplus

American Graffiti: hot dogs, hamburgers, Mel's Diner food

Kung Fu flicks: Chinese takeout

Tarzan films: exotic fruits, bananas, pineapples

Lawrence of Arabia: kabobs and rice

Bible movies: loaves and fishes

Valley of the Dolls: bowls of Good & Plenty and

candies that look like pills
Classic Disney cartoons: movie-theater candy
Titanic: lobster, crabs, shrimp on ice, *lots and lots* of ice
James Bond: classy hors d'oeuvres, martinis
Pirates of the Caribbean: roasted fish and other seafood, tropical fruits
Hollywood Awards Show: full out—seven-course dinner; on the cheap—popcorn

Naming Your Food

For creative and fun finger food, use your imagination to match up what you serve with your theme. Here's an actual menu that was used at a recent party:

Big Fish course: The Last Salmon on Rye
Cold Cut Mountain
Caviar (Eating *Nemo*)
Miniature *Lord of the Onion Rings*
Rum *Pirates of the Caribbean*
Ice in *The Cooler*
Crispy Biscuits (C-Biscuits = *Seabiscuit*. They were English, what can I say?)

You can do this with almost any item. For example, take that plate of cream cheese–filled hot peppers you got in the frozen-food section of the Safeway and heated up in the oven. By various themes, they could be called:

Horror Demon Seeds
Kung Fu or *Harry Potter* Dragon Eggs

Western Mexican Firecrackers
Chicago Tommy Gun Bullets
Military Hand Grenades
Tarzan or *Planet of the Apes* Monkey Poop

You get the idea. Make little cards that say what you're calling each item. You can get a few sheets of plain white card stock at Kinko's and cut it into four-inch squares. Fold each square in half so it will stand up on its own like a place card. Print your brilliant name for the food on each one. Then just set them out by the food so your guests can swoon, coo, and delight at your insufferable cleverness.

And Drink!

QUOTE

"Come on, Oscar, let's you and me get drunk."

—Bette Davis as Margaret Elliot, speaking to her golden statuette in *The Star* (1952)

OK, maybe not drunk. But certainly a smidge tee-hee. We may rely on celebrities to get shit-faced and do spectacularly stupid things for our tabloid amusement, but that's not the atmosphere you want for your party. The alcohol provided is to be consumed, we hope, in moderation. The goal is to get your guests relaxed and convivial, not falling-down sloppy or vomiting in that urn with grandma's ashes.

Let's look at the possibilities:

Pitchers of pre-mixed drinks. Very easy. Very simple. Invent a new drink (or rename an old one) based on this year's frontrunner film. Call it your "signature drink" and let that shut up those whining about a lack of choice (and who also *won't* be invited next year).

Full bar with bartender. Very classy, very Oscars. Also very expensive. Insures that each guest will be able to enjoy their favorite cocktail and not be limited to something like a pre-mixed batch of mojitos, which, I have to tell you, is so 2006.

Wine on the counter. Very *Sideways*. Very yuppie and very simple. It's the chic way to straddle the line between cheap and simple while still delivering a dash of easy elegance. If you buy red, you won't even have to bother with chilling it.

Fridge full of beer. Very *Smoky and the Bandit*. Very Super Bowl. Very casual, homey, and cheap. Hell, make it a kegger. Just make sure you have enough bathrooms for the mad dash during the commercial breaks and Irving Thalberg Memorial Award presentations.

You will be pleased to know that the majority of the money I was paid for writing this book was put into "liquid research." At least that's what I'm claiming on my taxes. In any event, the results are the delicious adult beverages I've listed below.

Recipe Time!

While you can certainly prepare and pour any drink you feel like serving, consider beverages that reflect the Oscar theme. You might be surprised to learn that there already exist mixed drinks that actually have Oscar-winner names.

APOCALYPSE NOW

INGREDIENTS:

⅓ oz. dry vermouth
⅓ oz. Irish cream liqueur
⅓ oz. tequila

PREPARATION:

Pour the dry vermouth and tequila into a shot glass. Stir well. Slowly pour the Irish cream liqueur on top.

GLADIATOR

INGREDIENTS:

½ oz. amaretto
½ oz. peach liqueur
2 oz. Sprite or 7-Up
2 oz. orange juice

-PREPARATION:

Pour the two liqueurs into a shot glass. Drop the shot glass into an old-fashioned glass or other lowball glass filled with the orange juice and Sprite or 7-Up.

MANHATTAN

INGREDIENTS:

1 ¼ oz. Canadian whiskey

½ oz. sweet vermouth

2–3 dashes Angostura bitters

Maraschino cherry for garnish

PREPARATION:

Pour the ingredients into a mixing glass with ice cubes. Stir well. Strain into a chilled cocktail glass. Garnish with cherry.

MIDNIGHT COWBOY

INGREDIENTS:

2 oz. bourbon

1 oz. dark rum

½ oz. heavy cream

PREPARATION:

Pour the ingredients into a mixing glass with ice cubes. Shake. Strain into a chilled cocktail glass.

THE GODFATHER

INGREDIENTS:

7/10 Scotch whiskey

3/10 amaretto

PREPARATION:

Put ice into glass. Add ingredients. Serve undecorated.

AMERICAN BEAUTY

INGREDIENTS:

1 oz. brandy

½ oz. dry vermouth

¼ tsp. white crème de menthe

1 oz. orange juice
1 tsp. grenadine
½ oz. tawny port

PREPARATION:

Pour all ingredients except the port into a mixing glass with ice cubes. Shake. Strain into a chilled cocktail glass. Carefully float the port on top.

APOLLO 13

INGREDIENTS:

2 oz. white rum
2 oz. fresh cream
½ oz. Grand Marnier
½ oz. Galliano
Dash of grenadine
Maraschino cherry for garnish

PREPARATION:

Pour the ingredients into a mixing glass with ice cubes. Shake. Strain into a chilled cocktail glass. Garnish with maraschino cherry.

AVIATOR

INGREDIENTS:

1 ¼ oz. gin
¼ oz. maraschino liqueur
Juice of 1 lemon
Pinch of sugar (optional)

PREPARATION:

Pour the ingredients into a mixing glass with ice cubes. Shake. Strain into a chilled cocktail glass.

THE FRENCH CONNECTION

INGREDIENTS:

2 oz. brandy

1 oz. amaretto

Splash triple-sec

PREPARATION:

Fill rocks glass with ice. Add brandy and amaretto and stir. Strain into a chilled cocktail glass. Top with a splash of triple-sec.

RAGING BULL (Warning: Dangerous!)

INGREDIENTS:

½ oz. Kahlua

½ oz. sambuca

PREPARATION:

Pour the Kahlua into a shot glass. Top with the Sambuca. Light on fire. Drink it quickly through a straw before it melts. Note: Do not try to pick up glass.

THE BIG CHILL

INGREDIENTS:

1 ½ oz. dark rum

1 oz. coconut cream

1 oz. orange juice

1 oz. cranberry juice

1 oz. apple juice

Pineapple wedge and maraschino cherry for garnish

PREPARATION:

Pour the ingredients into a mixing glass with ice cubes. Shake well. Strain into a chilled pilsner glass. Garnish with the pineapple wedge and maraschino cherry.

BLUE VELVET

INGREDIENTS:

1 oz. black raspberry liqueur
1 oz. melon liqueur
4 oz. vanilla ice cream
1 cup crushed ice
Dash blue curaçao
½ oz. whipped cream
Maraschino cherry for garnish

PREPARATION:

Pour the ingredients into a blender. Blend until smooth. Pour into a chilled parfait glass. Top with the blue curaçao, followed by the dab of whipped cream. Garnish with the maraschino cherry.

THE GREEN MILE

INGREDIENTS:

⅓ vodka
⅓ peach schnapps
⅓ lime juice
Drop of green food coloring

PREPARATION:

Put a drop of green food coloring in a shot glass. Add vodka and schnapps and lime juice.

THE LORD OF THE RINGS (Warning: This is hangover city, only drink one all night!)

INGREDIENTS:

3 oz. Jack Daniels
2 oz. Jim Beam
2 oz. dry gin

2 oz. vodka
3 oz. melon juice

PREPARATION:

Fill a large beer mug half full of ice. Combine liquor
in glass. Top with melon juice and stir only very
slightly. Note: Say no to any other booze for the night.

"Whoever Keyser Soze is, I can tell you he is going to get gloriously drunk tonight."

—Kevin Spacey accepting his Best
Supporting Actor award for
The Usual Suspects (1995)

And although these aren't quite exactly directly Oscar-linked, but given their names, they had to be included here:

HOLLYWOOD *(with a name like that, how could you resist?)*

INGREDIENTS:

1 oz. vodka
1 oz. Chambord
Pineapple juice

PREPARATION:

Pour the vodka and Chambord into any style glass
over ice. Add pineapple juice to fill.

RUBY SLIPPER *(I'm queer, so sue me.)*

INGREDIENTS:

  1 oz. Crown Royal
  Sprite or 7-Up
  Grenadine

PREPARATION:

  Half-fill a plastic cup with the Sprite or 7-Up. Add dash of grenadine. Pour Crown Royal into a shot glass. Drop shot in cup.

SCARLETT O'HARA

INGREDIENTS:

  2 oz. Southern Comfort
  6 oz. cranberry juice
  Dash of fresh lemon juice

PREPARATION:

  Combine ingredients in a highball glass over ice. Top with a dash of lemon juice.

LESBIAN ENCOUNTER *(close enough to* Girl, Interrupted *and* Color Purple *for me)*

INGREDIENTS:

  Combine equal parts:
  Melon liqueur
  Peach schnapps
  Banana liqueur
  Blue curaçao
  Cranberry juice
  Lime juice
  Splash of Sprite or 7-Up

PREPARATION:

Combine to taste in large pitcher. Serve by the shot.

Naming Your Poison

If you have an old favorite you'd prefer to serve, go ahead. For this evening you can rename it anything you want. For instance:

A dirty martini becomes A *Dirty Harry* Martini
A margarita becomes A Charlize Theron
   Monster Margarita
A cosmopolitan becomes A Hillary Swank *Boys
   Don't Cry* Cosmo
A whiskey sour becomes Dances With Whiskey
Any generic cocktail becomes A Philip
   Seymour Hoffman *Capote* Cocktail

Tie the name of your *cocktail du jour* into this year's nominees however the hell you like, it's your party.

"I Don't Know What to Buy"

If you don't know what to get because you're not a big drinker or need to limit expenses, don't worry. Just buy several bottles of sparkling wine and call it "The Bubbly" all night. It'll help everyone pretend you're all drinking the same champagne as the stars.

Yeah, right.

The Non-Alcoholic Stuff

Q
QUOTE
"I don't drink."

—Robert Duvall as Frank Burns in
*M*A*S*H* (1970)

Fair enough. Not everyone embraces the demon rum. Not only that, but some people will be driving home and therefore, we hope, choose to refrain. So buy sodas, tea, juice, milk, Ovaltine, Nestlé's Quick, whatever will make you and your thirsty guests happy and, preferably, look festive doing it.

If you're a nondrinker—for whatever reason—I don't wish to seem judgmental. I have dear friends in 12-Step programs of every ilk, so I don't make light of a person's choice not to drink. That said, forcing your convictions on others may not be a party "Do," so consider having alcohol available for them if not for you. That way everyone can make their own adult decision about imbibing. Just a thought.

In the meantime, here are a few non-alcoholic drinks with Hollywood-related names you might feel good about serving:

ROY ROGERS *(he was never nominated, but still a part of Hollywood history)*

INGREDIENTS:

6 oz. cola (or to fill)

Dash grenadine

Orange slice and maraschino cherry for garnish

PREPARATION:

Fill Collins or highball glass with ice. Add cola and grenadine. Garnish with orange slice and maraschino cherry.

SHIRLEY TEMPLE *(received a special miniature Oscar at the age of 6)*

INGREDIENTS:

6 oz. Sprite or 7-Up (or to fill)

1 oz. cherry mix

Maraschino cherry for garnish

PREPARATION:

Fill Collins or highball glass with ice. Add Sprite or 7-Up and cherry mix. Garnish with maraschino cherry.

CHICAGO LEMONADE (DRINK THIS AND YOU'LL STILL REMEMBER THE LYRICS TO "ALL THAT JAZZ")

INGREDIENTS:

1 oz. 7-Up

Juice of 1 lemon

1 oz. soda water

¾ oz. simple syrup

PREPARATION:

Combine ingredients in a highball over ice. Garnish with a lemon slice.

If you still wish to have no alcohol at your party, you're a brave soul and props to you. I suggest you tell everyone, "Today is my 90-day anniversary of being sober!" That'll not only shut up the complainers kvetching about there being no hooch, but they'll be forced to congratulate you.

And if your Oscar party is strictly for your AA buddies, may I suggest a *Leaving Las Vegas* theme? Your sponsor will love it.

The Drink That Says "Go Home"

After they've handed out the Best Actor and Actress awards, it's time to start serving the coffee. This is a little-known party ploy that lets your guests know the evening is about to end, but does it in a way so gracious that they actually like it. They'll stay for Best Director and, of course, Best Picture. And as soon as you've distributed your award gifts they'll be ready to leave your place in droves. You'll have your home back within 15 minutes of awarding the prize to whoever came in last place in the balloting.

Ooh, Did Someone Mention "Prizes" and "The Balloting"?

Yes, my dear, we did. By this point you've got a theme, the décor is happening, and we've addressed the issues of food and drink. We'll turn to Oscar balloting soon enough (in Chapter Six). But while we're still here in the area of procuring the things we need to pull off this party, it's time to talk about stuff you'll be giving away.

Namely swag bags and prizes!

Shortest and Longest

In Hollywood size matters. Just ask King Kong. Fortunately for the rest of us, "short" and "long" can also refer to how much time it takes to do whatever it is you're doing so lovingly and so well that you get nominated for an award for the way do it. See if you can answer these eight questions in short order:

1. What is the longest Best Picture winner?

2. What is the shortest Best Picture winner?

3. In terms of onscreen time, what was the shortest performance to win a Best Supporting Actor Oscar?

4. In terms of onscreen time, what was the shortest performance ever to win an Oscar?

Shortest and Longest

5. Who is the only actor or actress to win an Academy Award for a one-word role?

6. Who holds the record for the longest Oscar acceptance speech?

7. Who holds the record for the shortest Oscar acceptance speech?

8. What was the longest Academy Awards show ever?

CHAPTER FIVE

Prizes and Swag Bags

> "I bet they didn't tell you that was in the gift bag."
>
> —Adrien Brody, after deeply smooching a surprised Halle Berry who presented his Best Actor award for *The Pianist* (2002)

YES, YOU cheap bastard, that's *prizes*—plural. You can't have just one big blowout prize. Why? Let me walk you through this.

If you have 25 people at your party and only one wins, you now have 24 people who lost, got no prize, are possibly drunk by now, and pissed off at losing. This is not good. At your Oscar party, everybody wins! OK, true, some win more than others—that is, after all, the point of a competition. But remember, we're recreating the Hollywood experience here! Even though we're doing it on a Hoboken budget.

Smiles, everyone, smiles!

For each competition, whether the Oscar balloting or any of the other exciting competitions you'll discover in ensuing chapters, you need a prize that people desire so they'll want to win. For the Oscar balloting you also need a second- and possibly third-place prize, a loser prize for the person who scored the lowest points, and swag bags for everyone else to mollify them for spending five hours they'll never get back watching the awards show at your house. It sounds like a lot, but we can get creative.

The Balloting Prizes

The top prize needs to be something cool that your guests will covet the moment they learn what it is. Typically the package is built around the year's hottest or most stylish movie on DVD. It may or may not be up for an award, but that doesn't matter. It's all about style, presentation, and making everyone else jealous.

The second- and third-prize packages need to go downhill from that fast. Keeping in the last-year's-movie-on-DVD vein, second prize would be the film that was interesting in a gay sort of way, but not the most exciting movie. Examples of "interesting in a gay sort of way" would be a gay star, an out director, or homo-friendly storyline.

It doesn't even have to be a film from the most recent year. In the giddy excitement surrounding your party and the overeager desire to please, just be careful you don't confuse your gay-friendly movie titles. For instance:

This Movie, Yes! This Movie, No

YES	NO
Brokeback Mountain	Escape to Witch Mountain
The Adventures of Priscilla	The Adventures of Pluto Nash
Gods and Monsters	Gods and Generals
My Own Private Idaho	Private Parts
Tales of the City	Tales from the Crypt
The Boys in the Band	Boyz N the Hood
A Wedding Banquet	A Wedding on Walton's Mountain
Philadelphia	Munich

If all this has weakened your confidence in selecting prize-worthy party, there's another route you can take. Get stuff other than actual movies. Radical, I know, but it can and possibly should be considered. Especially if you're too big a wussy to walk into a video store and emerge a few short hours later with adequate prize materials.

Craptastic Movie Stuff!

There is a ton of this *sheis* available. You can use it for prizes or, if your budget is generous, for your swag bags. If you don't have the horror of a Spencer's Gifts store in your local mall, you can get this stuff on line. Be creative and mix-and-match for optimal kitsch value.

Trophies

No, they don't look exactly like Oscar awards, but they're in the ballpark and it's the best you can do. You'd think look-alike knockoff Oscar awards would be as easily available as look-alike knockoff Oscar gowns, but they're not. That's because the Academy guards its name, likenesses, and Oscar image like a certain action star… never mind. I'm not going there.

But these fake trophies run about ten bucks each, and when you give them out at your Oscar party, people understand what they're supposed to be. If you purchase it far enough in advance, you can even have something witty inscribed on the base: "Sees Way Too Many Movies," "Desperately Needs a Life," or "Only Man You're Going Home With."

Or, as I said, something witty.

Posters

Unless you live in Los Angeles, you'll probably have to go online, but you can easily get posters of the Hollywood sign, sights in Hollywood, Beverly Hills, your favorite stars, and your fave movies including, usually, the big money-making nominees. More arcane, rare, and vintage posters will cost you, but the ones we're talking about here go for around $8 to $15.

Standups

No, not comedians. These are cardboard "lifesize" cutouts with a folding cardboard stand attached in the back so they will—duh!—stand up. You can get these images portraying a variety of Hollywood personalities and, in some cases, characters (as long as you're not looking too far beyond the *Star Wars* world). You won't find this year's nominees, but if all you're going for is a general Hollywood feel, by all means knock yourself out. These puppies are a tad more pricey than the posters because you're paying royalties on them. They're typically in the $30 to $35 apiece range.

Film Cans

While perhaps the most famous film can is the one attached to Jennifer Lopez, these cans have that unmistakable shiny, new Tinseltown cachet that will serve your prize-gifting well. Available in silver or gold, they make excellent decorations and cool gift boxes just by themselves. At just under 11 inches in diameter and 1 ¾ inches thick, they can easily hold a couple of standard-sized DVDs, too. You can have your first, second, third, and loser prize DVDs in these film cans, on ostentatious display near the TV but kept a mystery until you reveal the prizes after the Oscar telecast.

"Why," you ask, "do I need to get a film can for my DVD prizes?" The answer is simple: because presentation is *everything*. If you really want to wow 'em, get film cans that were actually used to store film. They're not as sparkly-shiny, but they're the real deal and run about the same amount as the freshly minted faux cans, between $7 and $9. Such a bargain!

Caps

You can get black baseball-style caps that say "Producer," "Director," "Actor," "Actress," "Crew," and, our favorite, "Stuntman." The words are embroidered in white, and the caps run around $15 each. If caps are going to be part of your prize package (provided you don't want 'em yourself to walk around all cool at your own party), I'd suggest "Producer" for the first prize, "Director" for second, "Actor" for third, while the loser gets "Crew" only because they don't have a hat that says "Craft Services." Oh, and despite the Academy, it's politically correct to call a female performer an "actor." Alternately the caps may be considered desirable enough to be your entire set of prizes.

Miscellaneous Tchotchkes

There are mugs with the Hollywood Walk of Fame emblazoned on them, or with cameras and clapboards. There are shot glasses, maps to the stars' homes, movie stills, LA street and freeway signs, and all kinds of other crapola for your prize packages. Have fun with it.

Where to Buy This Glitzy Garbage:

HOLLYWOOD SOUVENIRS
(www.hollywoodsouvenirs.com)
6800 Hollywood Blvd.
Hollywood, CA 90028
(323) 962-8851

HOLLYWOOD MEGA STORE
(www.hollywoodmegastore.com)
940 West Washington Blvd.
Los Angeles, CA 90015
(213) 747-9239

Or search online. At iparty.com you can find pre-packaged Black Tie Party Packs and even Hollywood

Party Packs, and other online places have similar stuff. Or you may find a local store that you can actually visit and walk out with your precious prizes. That way, you don't have to wait for some cockamamie store in la-la land to send it through the mail. Especially since we all know how reliable the U.S postal service is.

Swag Bags

"Remember, ladies and gentlemen, nobody goes home empty-handed tonight. The losers all receive the new Oscar home game."

—Johnny Carson, hosting the 48th Annual Academy Awards

The Oscar presenters all come away from the telecast with their assistants in tow burdened down, as any assistant should be, with tens of thousands of dollars' worth of free, utterly unmerited goodies called "swag." It's the American way: giving rich people who don't need a thing tons of free and otherwise horribly expensive gifts just for showing up. God, what a country! It's how they keep the actors who didn't merit a nomination (perhaps because they sucked, perhaps because they didn't get *work*) from leaving the Kodak Theater feeling bummed, left out, and, God forbid, *ordinary*.

You, too, want to make sure no one leaves your party feeling lesser-than just because they were too boneheaded to win a simple competition. That's why I recommend you supply all guests with swag bags. It makes everybody feel special, plus it has some of that Hollywood-awards-ceremony feel. But how do you go about doing this?

Assemble the Bags

Step one is to come up with the bags themselves. Fancy always looks good. Naturally you don't want to raise expectations unduly by putting a piece of cheap movie candy in a bag that looks like it should hold Harry Winston jewelry. That's a recipe destined to disappoint. Let the quality of what you plan to give out dictate the bag it comes in.

How Many Bags Should You Get?

Estimate how many people will attend. Increase that number by 20 percent. Buy, assemble, and fill that many bags. By all means you want to avoid the embarrassment of not having enough. Keep that in mind when budgeting these items.

If disaster strikes and more people than expected show up, do some quick favor-asking of your friends. Explain the sitch to your close buds and ask them to forgo the swag bags tonight so that others can have them. If they really are your friends, they'll do that for you. If not, try bribing them. And if that doesn't work, never speak to them again. Any friendship that can be broken over a bag of cheap Hollywood stuff and candy isn't worth it, and you should post those compromising pictures you have of them on the Internet tomorrow.

But enough about that—let's fill those bags, huh? (Note: If you're running short of time, you may need to skip directly to Swag Bag Source #2.)

Swag Bag Source #1

This is the #1 place to start because:

- It actually helps your friends and acquaintances.
- It gives you interesting and varied items for your bags.
- It gives your guests something to use after your party, and thereby think of you, and your fabulous party, all over again.
- And it's free, free, free!

What is this marvelous source? The people you know! The only caveat is that you do have to invite them to your party. But your first stop on the Swag Bag Express is to visit them and ask 'em for stuff. Almost everybody has something they're selling. All you have to do is ask them for samples or gift cards and coupons for the goods and services they sell. Don't be shy. They *want* to give you these things—although sometimes *you* have to tell them why.

So here's why:

- It's an opportunity to introduce their product to a new group of people.
- It makes them look generous.
- They can network by talking up their product at your party.
- Since they'll be at your party, they'll get a bag with other people's freebies.

Keep in mind that there's a trust factor involved in asking for donations of this kind. Do not abuse the privilege by asking for 500 samples of Jose Ebert shampoo if you're only having 50 people. Remember, your donor will be at your party, will notice, think unkindly of you, and the next time you come in for a tint he'll burn the shit out of your hair. And if Tom the hunky bartender-owner of Nipples gives you 50 free-drink tickets, they'd better be in the bags, because if they're not and you keep showing up at happy hour with 'em, there will be something in your gin and tonic besides gin and tonic. Be honest about what you're doing.

The people you should think about asking for free swag include:

- Friends
- Clients
- People you'd *like* to be your friends and clients
- Your friends' friends
- Family (and their friends and clients)
- Neighbors
- Nearby businesses

If you're feeling inspired and want to branch out beyond this list, walk up to any business whose donation would help round out your swag. Some businesses to consider hitting up:

- Bars
- Clubs
- Gyms
- Hair salons
- Tanning salons
- Apparel stores
- Local erotic emporium
- Coffeehouses
- Personal trainers/coaches
- Restaurants
- Ice-cream parlors
- Movie theaters
- Video rental
- Music stores
- Arts organizations
- Museums
- Pet stores
- Car washes
- Florists
- Gift stores
- Jewelers
- Massage therapists
- Tattoo artists
- Hardware stores

You're limited only by your imagination, willingness to pursue a vendor, and time. Remember, doll, there are other things you need to do to prepare.

Oh, and don't forget to make a written list of all the nice people and businesses who gave free goodies. That way, you'll remember (1) who to thank so they'll feel like helping you out again; and (2) who to hit up for your next swag bags!

Swag Bag Source #2

Just because this is source #2 does *not* make it the lesser source. You may not have time or inclination to pursue all the people and vendors from source #1. There's no shame in that. In fact, even if you did get a bunch of swag from vendors, I recommend rounding it out with stuff from this source.

What is this source? The store. You're going to have to—gulp—buy it. But I'll show you how.

Go to a party store. They always have gift bags because even mothers of four-year-olds know that a birthday party means that every caterwauling brat has to go home with a gift bag or else catches hell about it from every mother who dragged their demon spawn to it. At the party store you'll find a selection of bags to fill.

If your town is bereft of a party store, consider moving. Seriously. who wants to live where a body can't even make a living helping other people be festive? But if you don't have time to move before Oscar night, get a bundle of lunch bags from the grocery and tart them up. Make a star stencil and spraypaint the bags. Staple a bit of feather boa to the top. Use spray glue and throw glitter at 'em. Heck, do *something*. Use your imagination, for God's sake.

Filling Your Bags on the Cheap

Who cares if it's cheap? If you want to make somebody's face light up, just hand 'em a bag of free crap. People just flat out *love*. getting giveaway stuff, no matter how 99¢ store it may feel to you. It's unexpected and therefore a treat. So don't feel bad because you can't put $500 worth of quality swag in each person's bag. It's not about the money, it's about the fun—*always*. Well, that and a week later hearing back from someone how fabulous they heard your party was. But that's fun, too!

At the party store (remember, you were there getting the bags?) spend a while looking around at what they have. Most will have items for sale that sadly represent a straight person's interpretation of Hollywood. Pick up a few. Remember to buy enough to put one in every bag. Because if Patty's swag bag doesn't have the cool item that Jon's does, Patty will be going home with a big bag of bitter. Avoid that.

Don't get all wrapped up in trying to make every single item in your swag bags reflect your theme or the nominated movies. That's a surefire way to make yourself crazy and spend way too much time on this. As long as you think "Festive!" you'll be on the right track. And if something does reflect your theme and/or nominated movies, it's gravy!

Here are some swag bag–worthy items I saw during a random visit to my neighborhood party store:

Plastic leis
Mylar foil wigs
Plastic sunglasses
Tiaras
Clappers
Stickers
Groucho glasses
Maze puzzles
Plastic rings
Packs of playing cards
Party poppers
Whoopee cushions
Fuzzy pens
Chinese fans
Glowsticks
Key rings
Rubber duckies
Beads
Congratulation ribbons
Bubbles
Winners trophies

WARNING: If you include potentially messy items like bubbles or Silly String, guests will stain your suede sofa with spilled bubble juice and you'll be picking Silly String out of the chandelier, grand piano, and bushes for months.

While you're at the play store, wander around in aisles you might not think of as pertinent. Mardi Gras is around this time of year, and that means you'll find fun beads in that area. People love Mardi Gras beads—who cares that it has nothing to do with Oscar? The new-baby section may have stuff that you can use or associate with a nominated film. In the wedding section you'll find tiny photo frames for a buck each for great swag bag filler. Check out the baby-shower area for a *Raising Arizona*, *Look Who's Talking*, or even *Rosemary's Baby* party haul.

And at the low end, you can always fill (or add to) your swag bags with movie-theater candy. Search online to order the harder-to-find things like Cinnamon Stinky Feet or Swedish Fish, but typically you'll find enough movie-theater candy at the grocery, such as:

Hershey Bars	Lemonheads	Twizzlers
Baby Ruths	M&M's	Whoppers
Boston Baked Beans	Reese's Pieces	Zagnuts
	Reese's Peanut Butter Cups	Cracker Jacks
Almond Joys		Gum
Butterfingers	Mr. Goodbars	Pez
Fifth Avenues	O'Henrys	Junior Mints
Heath Bar	Paydays	Good & Plenty's
Goobers	Rice Crispy Treats	Hot Tamales
York Peppermint Patties		SweetTarts
	Skittles	Milk Duds
Gummy Bears	Starbursts	Raisinets
Jolly Ranchers	Twix	
KitKats	Tootsie Rolls	

And there's always popcorn. And bags of piñata candy. If candy is all you can afford to hand out, *do not be ashamed*. Hold your head up high. Laugh about it. Make it a "thing." In fact, make that the *point*. Remember, *it's all about how you present it*. Just like the studios in Hollywood, if you put a good face on it and never back down, the public will buy it without question. With style, flair, and brazen balls, you can pull anything off.

When Do I Dole Out the Swag?

At the end of the evening, of course. It's like the cherry on top of the parfait—the perfect capper. Don't tell people it's coming, let it be a surprise. Enjoy the squeals of delight from your guests.

Whatever the hell you hand out, everyone will leave clutching a bag of something they didn't have when they came in. Trust me, people will be thrilled. You will have made your guests Hollywood-happy. Your party will be talked about for weeks.

And the word for that is: "success"!

Q Facts #1: Buying and Selling Oscar

Industry experts speculate that 150 Oscars have been sold since the first Academy Awards in 1929. In the past, when Academy Award winners or their heirs fell on hard times, an Oscar might find its way to an auction house and anyone who had the money could buy it outright. Shocking! Thank God nothing that crassly commercial happens in Hollywood between studios, huh?

The first one came up for auction in 1949. The

Academy didn't like that one bit, so they devised a "Winner's Agreement" that is now standard. When you win an Oscar, before they will engrave your name on it, the Academy makes you sign this contract in the blood of a newborn infant. OK, maybe not in blood, but they're not fooling around. It says that you agree "not to sell or otherwise dispose of" your Oscar statuette without first offering to sell it to the Academy for one buck.

They can't stop the sale of every statue. Oscars awarded before 1949 may be bought and sold on the open market. Every so often a post-1950 Oscar will get traded on the "gray market." But the Academy says they'll object whenever one comes up for sale and to "throw legal impediments in the way at every opportunity."

A few recent Academy Award sales:

- Steven Spielberg purchases Clark Gable's 1934 Oscar for *It Happened One Night* for $607,500 to protect it from further commercial exploitation. He doesn't keep it for himself, but generously returns it to the Academy. Suckup!
- Michael Jackson buys the Best Picture Oscar for *Gone With the Wind* for $1.54 million. God knows what he did with it.
- Spielberg drops $580,000 for Bette Davis's 1938 Best Actress Academy Award for *Jezebel*. He returns it to the Academy. Boring!
- Kevin Spacey pays $156,875 for the Oscar won by composer George Stoll in 1945 for *Anchors Aweigh*. Like Spielberg, Spacey returns it to the Academy. Copycat.

- Spielberg shells out $207,500 for Bette Davis's other Oscar, the one awarded in 1935 for *Dangerous*. He returns it to the Academy. Jeez, don't you wish he'd have mounted it on the hood of his Bentley, put it in the front yard like a lawn jockey, or combined it with his own and used them as bowling pins?
- Magician David Copperfield forks over $232,000 for Michael Curtiz's 1943 Best Director award for *Casablanca*. He keeps it on display in his bedroom. Can't you just see him breaking it out when he has a lady friend over? "Wanna see me make this disappear? I'll need a volunteer from the audience…" One word: "Ew!"

CHAPTER SIX

The Ballot

"I guess this proves that there are just as many nuts in the Academy as anywhere else."

—Jack Nicholson, accepting his Best Actor award for *One Flew Over the Cuckoo's Nest* (1975)

THE CENTERPIECE of Oscar party action is, of course, the ballots. Ya gotta have 'em. It makes everyone feel like they're a part of the ceremony, which, of course, they are not. But movies are all about dreams and special effects and denial, so for this one night, you and your guests are Hollywood insiders. Having full ballots of all the Oscar nominees for your privileged party participants is the "special effect" that helps create that.

Please note that I said "*full* ballots." If you have only partial ballots for the big awards, you will guarantee great lulls in interest, if not outright boredom, during the lesser awards. After all, if they only care about, say, the top ten awards because that was all your ballot included, those are the only awards to which they will pay any attention. If they have no stake in Best Short Documentary or Best Achievement in Sound Mixing, they're sure to get fidgety during those presentations and start looking about for mischief?

I can tell you from personal experience that you do *not* want people's attention to stray from the point of your party, because if guests get bored, they will:

- Wonder what you were thinking when you chose that kitchen wallpaper.
- Notice that the crudités look tired and need replenishing. And so does the host.
- Traipse down the hall to the loo and root around in your medicine cabinet for recreational Klonopin.
- Wander into off-limits rooms to snoop for "private photos" in your sock drawer.
- Use your office extension to call friends in Brazil.

No, no, no. You must keep their eyes on the prize by giving them a *full and complete* ballot of *all* the Oscar nominations.

And it is so simple to do. You don't have to go tracking down the info from *Daily Variety*. You don't even have to transcribe it. The very kind and glamorous web geeks at the Academy have already put it online for you. Just go to www.oscar.com (duh!), click on "Nominees," and—ta-dah!—there it is.

If you want to do special stuff with it, like add graphics (hmm, shirtless photos of all the Best Actors? Sexy shots of the leading ladies? Posters of the films?), go for it. It's your life to waste.—I mean "enjoy." But there you have the basic, bare requirements for sustaining people's interest during the entire awards show.

Assigning Point Values: Up the Ante!

Again, this is all about maintaining interest. More than that, it's about building and heightening the delicious tension as the evening progresses.

Prior to the telecast, create a sheet listing all the awards with a point value for each. (We'll go into that in a minute.) Display it by the TV, next to the booze, or wherever it will be seen by the most people. (OK, next to the booze.) The point is to let everybody know how the ballots are going to be tallied. This does two things.

First, it provides full disclosure of the scoring process, thus preventing ugly fights. For instance, say Sally wins in the balloting over Brenda. Although Brenda got more *awards* right, Sally scored the most *points* because she got the big awards right and they're worth more points. Knowing the points process keeps Brenda from getting angry and calling Sally an evil two-headed cheating slut-bitch and a carrier of lesbian bed-death, thus bringing awkwardness into the evening.

Second, it increases Oscar-focused excitement as you head into the big awards near the end of the show. For some reason, this is something that many straight people don't understand and therefore overlook, at least at the parties I've attended. Increasing the point value is done here for the same reason as on *Jeopardy!* If you suck in one round, the next one is worth more points so you have a chance to pull ahead of the current frontrunner. Even Merv Griffin figured that one out.

If you've weighted the awards that come later in the evening with more points, it's possible that the person who got only the Best Animated Short Film and Best Foreign Language Film (one lousy point each, ho-hum) could still hit it big or even win by getting the Best Actor and Best Film right. That person is going to stay avidly interested. The worst thing that guy or gal is going do is snarf up all the bridge mix out of nerves. It keeps the largest number of guests "in the game" for the longest time.

Now let's talk about the points. You're welcome to assign points any way you want. But this is my book, so I recommend:

- Best Film: 7 points
- Best Director: 5 points
- Best Actress and Best Actor: 5 points each
- Best Supporting Actress and Best Supporting Actor: 3 points each
- Your Choice: just to mix it up a little, say Best Cinematography and Best Song: 2 points each
- Everything else: 1 point each

The producers of the Oscar telecasts like to shake things up from year to year, but generally they start off with the Best Supporting Actress and Actor. They do that so viewers will tune in at the beginning instead of waiting until 1:00 a.m. when the show is usually only just getting around to the awards Middle America gives a rat's ass about. The great thing about this is, it starts out your ballot competition with a bang, giving some folks what appears to be a head start right out of the box.

You, however, savvy awards watcher that you are, know better. There are at least a couple of hours of nothing but one-point awards to slog through that could easily erase any lead held by those who got a Best Supporting award or two correct. You also know that the points your guests are building during this time can be completely upset by the more heavily weighted awards to come. Ah, yes, you know these things and you can enjoy watching your friends worry over what is to come. But…

They are only going to do that if the prize for winning is worth it. You *did* buy excellently fun prizes, right?

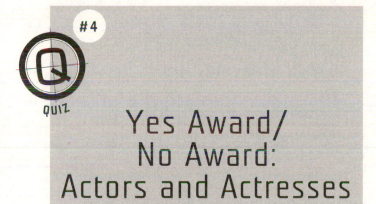

 # 4

Q

QUIZ

Yes Award/ No Award: Actors and Actresses

Guess which of these actors has won Academy Awards and which has not. You may be surprised!

Glenn Close
Denzel Washington
Luise Rainer
Peter O'Toole

Yes Award/ No Award: Actors and Actresses

Tom Cruise

Whoopi Goldberg

Jim Carrey

Harrison Ford

Morgan Freeman

Ronald Reagan

Judy Garland

Ernest Borgnine

Bette Midler

Meg Ryan

Anna Magnani

Debra Winger

Sean Connery

Albert Finney

Angela Lansbury

Benicio del Toro

Richard Burton

Faye Dunaway

Helena Bonham Carter

Judi Dench

Madeline Kahn

Peter Sellers

Bing Crosby

Ginger Rogers

Fred Astaire

CHAPTER SEVEN

Handicapping the Ballot

"The Golden Globes are fun. The Oscars are business."

—Warren Beatty

EVEN THOUGH you're the host, there's no reason you shouldn't enter the balloting competition. It's your party, and you should be able to enjoy that part of it, too. Just know that if you do win, you'll have to award the prize to the person who had the next-highest score. Otherwise, you'll not appear gracious, generous, or humble. You want people to look to you, smile, and think "How noble," not "What a fat, glistening prick," followed quickly by "I think I'll go piss on her towels."

Still and all, you do want to win. It's the American way. If nothing else you want to show your guests that you understand Oscar better than anyone else.

Prior Awards Shows

As far as you're concerned, the only reason other awards shows like the ones put on by the Directors Guild of America (DGA), Screen Actors Guild (SAG), screenwriters guild (WGA), etc., exist is to help you handicap the Oscars. The people and films they honor give *indications* as to who and what might win, but they should be taken as only part of a much broader picture.

The same goes for the Golden Globes and anything that comes out of the various film critics' awards. Often these organizations have a self-serving point to make, axes to grind, or some other agenda at work. And sometimes the voters were deprived of oxygen at birth or dropped on their heads as infants. It all goes into the mix.

Whatever.

So to give you an edge in picking your own Oscar winners, here's a category-by-category listing of considerations to help you sort through the aforementioned mix and mess.

Important Considerations by Category

Best Actor and Actress (leading and supporting):

We start with these categories because they have perhaps the most intriguing, and certainly the longest, list of variables. (I'm including the actors and actresses in supporting roles because the considerations also apply to them.) Generally the more of these the actor or actress has, the more likely he or she will go home with Oscar.

Please remember that these variables are not jokes. Each has historical Oscar precedent and the numbers to back it up. This is about winning, damn it.

Yeah, about that. We're here to learn how to develop expertise in predicting the winner—not who *should* win, and certainly not to rely on our intuition. So pay attention to these "positive" factors that sway Academy voters:

- Did the character have a heavy accent?
- Was the character a real historical person?
- Did the character age on screen?
- Was the character lesbian or gay?
- Has the actor/actress been overlooked in the past?
- Is the actor/actress old enough that Academy members might not get a chance to honor them at some future date?
- Is the actor/actress popular in Hollywood?
- Was the picture a "serious drama"?
- Was the performance over-the-top? (In Hollywood, that translates as "fine acting.")
- Did this actor get a Screen Actors Guild awards for their performance?
- Was the character "crippled" in some way (including, but not limited to: alcoholism (a biggie), deformity, quirky disease, fatal illness, and mentally, emotionally, or physically challenged)?
- Did the character die?

- Did the actor/actress die? (That's a shoo-in—unless they're foreigners. Sorry, Massimo Troisi.)

In addition to these considerations, there are a few things that can be separated out by gender. Factor these in, as well:

For Best Actress and Supporting Actress

- Was the role young?
- Was the character in entertainment?
- Was the character a prostitute?
- Was a beautiful actress made ugly by make-up and clothes?
- Did the character suffer terribly?
- Was the character a victim?

For Best Actor and Supporting Actor

- Was the film action-adventure?
- Was the character in the military or otherwise involved in some form of law and order?

And, of course, the "negative" factors:
- Any kind of subtlety whatsoever.
- Potty mouth. Academy members are older and they hate the "F" word.
- For men, a nomination for a romantic melodrama. Not one guy has won for that.

Best Visual Effects:

- Which one cost the most?

Best Documentary (feature or short):

- Was it about the Holocaust?
- Have you heard of it? If you have, chances are the Academy members have, too, and they vote for what's familiar to them.

Best Foreign Language Film:

- Have you heard of it?
- Which one had the biggest box office? It's a Hollywood truism that if it made a lot of money, it must be good. (Don't get me started.)

Best Animated Feature:

- Was it made by Pixar?
- Was it made by Nick Park?

Best Makeup:

- Is Rick Baker nominated?
- No? Flip a coin.

Best Costume Design:

- Which was the most flat-out showy and pretty? Remember, nothing here is about subtlety.

Best Original Song:

The Academy is a schizophrenic mess on this one. It's mostly made up of older members who like the safe crap, but every so often they like to appear "with it" by choosing something they think their grandkids might listen to. Trust me, Donald Sutherland does not ride around with "It's Hard Out Here for a Pimp" on replay. Which brings up the next problem in this category—songs that suck.

Every year Hollywood patches together a batch of unlikely tuneless drivel and looks away in shame as the nominees for Best Original Song are read. For example, in 1986, the nominees were "Glory of Love," "Life in a Looking Glass" (Anybody remember that? Anyone? Bueller?), "Mean Green Mother from Outer Space" (Christ, people, these are the Oscars!), "Somewhere Out There," and "Take My Breath Away." And what won? "Take My Breath Away." All of which leads to the only comment I can make about handicapping the Best Original Song: You're screwed.

Best Original Score:

- Did John Williams write it?
- OK, then, does it have a distinctive sound or, God forbid, a melody?

I know that may sound simplistic and dismissive, but Academy members tend to vote what they remember. Plus the largest branch of the Academy is the Actors Guild, and actors have tiny brains, most of which are consumed with thoughts only about themselves leaving damn little room for much else but a tune. (Can you tell I once dated an actor?)

Best Animated Short and Best Live Action Short:

Not even the Academy members know what to vote for here. Special showings of these are held in Hollywood and New York specifically for members so they'll have an informed opinion. And how many actually attend? Here's a hint: Don't expect to see Goldie and Kurt chomping popcorn in between taking notes. Doesn't happen. Academy members are going to vote just like you, by putting an X in the box next to the title they like the most.

Best Art Direction, Cinematography, Film Editing, Sound Editing, Sound Mixing, Visual Effects:

Each of these is voted on by the members of the union-slash-guild that is represented, not by the Academy at large. (There are a few others like that, direction for instance, but those we can handicap.) This means that professionals are doing the voting. The highly special-ized knowledge, talent, and craft for each of these fields are far beyond what you or I might think goes into it. After all, we don't even know the difference between sound editing and sound mixing. They do. They also know what to look or listen for and how to best judge each work, but we don't. So I can't help you here.

And quit yer bitchin' right now. If there weren't any wild cards in the mix, what fun would that be? It adds to the suspense, so get over it.

Best Original Screenplay and Adapted Screenplay:

- Has the writer been snubbed or overlooked in the past?
- Is the writer also up for Best Director so the Academy can pawn him off with this award

and give Best Director to someone they like better?

- Has the writer been nominated several times before so that this award could be a body-of-work award?
- Is there a buzz about the script? If two films are the ones vying for Best Picture and one is up for Original Screenplay and the other for Adapted Screenplay, the Academy will sometimes reward each with writing Oscars.
- Is the film "important"?
- Is it unlikely to get any other major award? A screenplay award is sometimes a pat-on-the-head acknowledgement so they can give the more prestigious award to the other big-buzz movie.
- Did it make a lot of money?
- Did the screenwriters guild give it any awards at their ceremony?

Best Director:

- Has the director been snubbed or over-looked in the past?
- Is the director well loved in Hollywood?
- Did the directors guild honor him or her at their ceremony?

And finally, the really big clincher, the last award of the evening that can completely change the outcome of everyone's ballot competition...

Best Picture:

- Did it make a lot of money?
- Is the picture's studio spending the most money pushing it?
- How did it do at the Golden Globes? (Important to consider, but not always an accurate indicator.)
- Is it "important"? Because an "important" film trumps lighter fare.
- Is it safe? Because safe trumps "important."
- Is it "important" and safe? Because that's a winner.

Other Means of Handicapping the Oscar Race

Read, read, read. Any and every source that can help you prognosticate is fair game. There are books galore on the subject that compare and contrast categories, winners, losers, and everything in between. These sources break down past Oscar races by every category you can think of (genre, gender, race, box office, etc.), factoring in the zeitgeist of the time, the political environment, and popularity. Here are a few you might want to consult:

All About Oscar: The History and Politics of the Academy Awards, by Emanuel Levy (published by Continuum). The author is an obsessive freak and film critic, which I realize is redundant, but I love him for being both. He's also a teacher so he has an

academic's approach to the research, and
really knows his stuff.

*The Big Show: High Times and Dirty Dealings
Backstage at the Academy Awards*, by Steve
Pond (published by Faber & Faber, Inc.).
This isn't going to be as much help with your
predictions as the others, but it's fun for the
juicy behind-the-scenes intrigue. Plus, it'll
give you lots of fun stories to regale your
guests with during commercials.

*Inside Oscar: The Unofficial History of the
Academy Awards*, by Mason Wiley and
Damien Bona (published by Ballantine
Books). At well over 1,100 pages, this is an
encyclopedic must-have for any movie fan.
It's packed with a blow-by-blow account of
every Oscar race from the first one through
1994. Who was nominated, how the studios
manipulated things, who won, what the
losers said and did, even the after-parties are
all there in delicious, gossipy style. Get this
book and its companion volume…

*Inside Oscar 2: 6 New Years of Academy Awards
History: 1995–2000*, by Damien Bona (sadly,
Mason Wiley passed away) (published by
Ballantine Books). This covers the years
indicated in the same fact-oriented yet juicy
way. And keep your eyes peeled for the next
installment because whenever it comes out,
you'll want to own that one, too.

*The Academy Awards: The Complete
Unofficial History*, by Gail Kinn and Jim

Piazza (published by Black Dog & Leven-
thal Publishers). Updated right after the
2006 awards, it's a great coffee-table book
of appealingly displayed facts and photos
to just happen to have lying about as your
guests arrive.

If you purchase these books, you might notice that
every one of them carries this disclaimer: "This book
is neither authorized nor endorsed by the Academy of
Motion Picture Arts and Sciences." Since the Academy
only prints, authorizes, or endorses books that are
flattering to itself, it's only the *unofficial* books like those
listed that provide anything approaching objective insight,
criticism, and most important, dish. If you simply must
have an officially sanctioned volume, try these two:

*75 Years of the Oscar: The Official History of
the Academy Awards*, by Robert Osborne
(published by Abbeville Press).
50 Designers/50 Costumes, forward by Jeffrey
Kurland, introduction by Deborah N. Landis
(published by the University of California Press). This one won't help you predict
an Oscar, but it's full of swoony photos of
Hollywood movie style.

A Final Word on the Balloting

The last inside-track tip I can offer for predicting this
year's Oscar race is to read *Entertainment Weekly* maga-
zine. The writers for this glossy pop-culture rag have

their smooching lips so far up the ass of everyone in Hollywood—God love 'em—that they've become pretty damn good at putting together an overview of how many people are favoring whom, and what, for which award. When it comes to marking your ballot, give substantial weight to whatever they predict for this year.

Q List #3:
Top 10 Oscar Speeches

#10:

"It's, uh, reassuring for me to look out at all of you and see how pretty and how lovely you look tonight. And so many gifted people are still making pictures like you do with your clothes on. And contrary to what Dustin Hoffman thinks, it is not an obscene evening, it is not garish, and it is not embarrassing."

—FRANK SINATRA, cohosting the
47th Annual Academy Awards

#9 (a two-parter):

"My dear colleagues, I thank you very much for this tribute to my work. I think that Jane Fonda and I have done the best work of our lives. And I salute you, and I pay tribute to you, and I think you should be very proud that in the last few weeks you've stood firm and you have refused to be intimidated by the threats of a small bunch

of Zionist hoodlums whose behavior...[booing from audience]...whose behavior is an insult to the stature of Jews all over the world and to their great and heroic record of struggle against fascism and oppression. And I pledge to you that I will continue to fight against anti-Semitism and fascism. Thank you."

—VANESSA REDGRAVE, accepting the
Best Supporting Actress for *Julia* (1977)

Followed a few minutes later by:

"I am sick and tired of people exploiting the occasion of the Academy Awards....I would like to suggest to Miss Redgrave that her winning an Academy Award is not a pivotal moment in history, does not require a proclamation, and a simple thank you would have sufficed."

—SCREENWRITER PADDY CHAYEFSKY,
presenting at the 50th Annual Academy Awards

#8:

"Oprah, Uma! Uma, Oprah!"

—DAVID LETTERMAN hosting the 67th Annual
Academy Awards, his only such gig

#7:

"I have invited my fellow documentary nominees on the stage with us, and we would like to—they're here in solidarity with me because we like nonfiction. We like nonfiction, and we live in fictitious times. We live in the

time where we have fictitious election results that elect a fictitious president. We live in a time where we have a man sending us to war for fictitious reasons. Whether it's the fiction of duct tape or fiction of orange alerts, we are against this war, Mr. Bush. Shame on you, Mr. Bush, shame on you. And any time you got the pope and the Dixie Chicks against you, your time is up. Thank you very much."

—MICHAEL MOORE, accepting his Best Documentary award for *Bowling for Columbine* (2002)

#6:

"If there's one thing that actors know—other than there weren't any WMDs—it's that there is no such thing as best in acting."

—SEAN PENN, accepting his Best Actor award for *Mystic River* (2003)

#5:

"I want to thank anyone who spends a part of their day creating. I don't care if it's a book, a film, a painting, a dance, a piece of theatre, a piece of music. Anybody, anybody who spends a part of their day sharing their experience with us. I think this world would be unlivable without art, and I thank you."

—STEVEN SODERBERGH, accepting his Best Director award for *Traffic* (2000)

#4:

"I'm king of the world!"

—JAMES CAMERON, humbly accepting the
Best Picture award for *Titanic* (1997)

#3:

*"Isn't it fascinating to think that probably the only laugh
that man will ever get in his life is by stripping off and
showing his shortcomings."*

—DAVID NIVEN, cohosting the
46th Annual Academy Awards after an
unexpected streaker jogged across the stage

#2:

*"Hello. My name is Sacheen Littlefeather. I'm Apache,
and I am president of the National Native American Affirmative Image Committee. I'm representing
Marlon Brando this evening, and he has asked me to
tell you, in a very long speech, which I cannot share
with you presently, because of time, but I will be glad
to share with the press afterward, that he very regret-
fully cannot accept this very generous award, and the
reasons for this being are the treatment of American
Indians today by the film industry...*[murmuring in
audience]*...excuse me...*[booing and applause]*...and
on television in movie reruns and also with the recent
happenings at Wounded Knee. I beg at this time that I
have not intruded upon this evening and that we will,
in the future...our hearts and our understanding will*

meet with love and generosity. Thank you on behalf of Marlon Brando."

—SACHEEN LITTLEFEATHER after Marlon Brando's Best Actor award for *The Godfather* (1972) is announced at the 45th Annual Academy Awards

#1:

"This means so much more to me this time, I don't know why. I think the first time I hardly felt it because it was all too new. But I want to say thank you to you. I haven't had an orthodox career, and I've wanted more than anything to have your respect. The first time I didn't feel it. But this time I feel it! And I can't deny the fact that you like *me! Right now you* like *me! Thank you!"*

—SALLY FIELD, accepting her second Best Actress award, this time for *Places in the Heart* (1984)

CHAPTER EIGHT

Other Fun Competitions

QUOTE

"Losing would suck."

—Ben Affleck, on his *Good Will Hunting* (1997) co-screenwriting nomination (He won.)

WHY DO you want a competition beyond the Oscar balloting? Lots of reasons. Now that the Oscars are on Sundays, you can make an entire day of it. You can serve (or go out for) brunch with friends and then gather in the den for games calculated to entertain, test each other's knowledge, and build excitement during the countdown to Oscar time.

On the West Coast, the awards are over at around 9:00 to 9:30 p.m. and the evening is still relatively young. You could use that time for competitions among the bitter-enders—those who stay at a party until the last possible moment. Doing that will certainly separate the hard-core fans from the regular folks, because for most people, the evening is over after the Best Picture award.

If your West Coast plans are for competition(s) *après* telecast, you'll need a pretty impressive prize to motivate people to stay. I suggest jewelry. Or real estate.

And if you're an East Coaster (or even one of those hot, meaty, corn-fed folks in the center of the country) looking to fill up the entire day with Oscar-related film folderol, why *not* have extra competitions? It makes the whole Academy Awards dealio an all-day event in your very own home. With you as the star. Yeah, *you*. Uh-huh.

Thought that'd get your attention.

Remember, I'm not saying that you must do all, or any, of these games and competitions. Hell, you don't have to do a damn thing. I'm just here to help you consider what you *might* do, to give you ideas about what it is *possible* to do, and how to do it so that you can wring the most enjoyment out of it before you and everyone else goes back to their sad little lives in the real world.

QUOTE

"Tell 'em 'game called on account of Oscar.'"

—Stephen Boyd as Frankie Fane in *The Oscar* (1966)

The Oscar Drinking Game

This couldn't be more simple—or popular. The only hard part is keeping up.

Take a swallow of your drink if:

- Joan Rivers misidentifies someone.
- The camera cuts to Jack Nicholson.
- An Oscar winner uses the words "blessed," "humbling," or "my agent."
- A presenter can't pronounce one of the nominees.

Take two swallows of your drink if:

- Anyone cries, whether onstage or in the audience.
- The orchestra cuts off an acceptance speech.
- A presenter can't read the teleprompter.
- An Oscar winner forgets to thank a significant other.

Drain your whole glass if:

- We get a juicy same-sex kiss.
- Somebody outs a star.
- A gay-themed movie wins Best Picture.

And to hell with alcohol poisoning, swig the whole damn bottle if:

- Somebody refuses an award. Hey, this is the Oscars, fer chrissakes!

Enjoy. Oh, and have a taxi cab ready to take your guests home. After all, you need 'em to get home alive so they can tell everyone how fabulous your Academy Awards party was.

Charades

I can already feel you rolling your eyes. "Puh-leaze!" you wail with impatience and annoyance, "charades are *sooo* sleepaway camp!" Well, if you'll remember, so was sexual discovery, and you didn't complain about that. My point is that charades remains a timeless and oddly fulfilling classic.

Don't start your evening off with charades, though, or your audience will have the same reaction you did five sentences back. The trick: *Wait until everyone's tipsy.* Then *everything* is funny!

Note: If you're going to play charades prior to the awards ceremony, start the game at least an hour before you want to sit down and pay attention to the show or pre-show. You do *not* want this cutting into the entire reason for the evening!

1. Before the party, get 20 slips of paper that look the same. On each one, write the name of a movie. Don't worry, we're not going to play 20 rounds of charades. Nine or 11 is about as much as a party can sustain. You want an odd number so there won't be a tie.

2. Fold all the slips of paper the same way and put them in a container. A Charlie Chaplin

derby would be fitting, but a Tupperware bowl will do.

3. When people start getting a bit tee-hee, announce that there will be a competition with prizes awarded, and that competition is…charades! Before anyone has a chance to make a sour face, tell them that the winning team gets the best seats for the Academy Awards pre-show and telecast.

4. Quickly divide the room up into two teams. That way, everyone is invested in getting the answer right as quickly as possible. Name your teams: The Jean Hersholts and the Irving Thalbergs; the Sharks and the Jets; the Bettes and the Joans. Don't let them come up with their own names because it'll take too long and you've got to get this ball rolling.

5. Whichever team is the fastest to tell you which movie got robbed of Best Picture in 2006 goes first. (*Brokeback Mountain,* in case you've forgotten!) That team, call them the Hersholts, chooses one of their own members to act out the charade.

6. That person goes to the front of both groups and picks a slip of paper with the name of a movie on it out of the Charlie Chaplain derby. (Or, God help us, that nasty Tupperware.) He or she must silently read the movie title on the paper so as not to allow anyone else to see it, and then act out the movie in charades style.

7. Both teams compete to get the correct name of the movie. You, as all-powerful host, get to determine which side said the correct name of the movie first and award the points. After that movie has been guessed correctly, the other team, in this case the Thalbergs, send a representative up to act out the next movie. Continue alternating between the two teams. And just to keep everyone on edge, it has to be a different person from each team every time.

8. Allow the winners to claim the best seats in your house for the Oscar show.

9. Shame the losers mercilessly.

QUOTE

"By the way, be sure to stay tuned for the whole show, because at the end of the night we are going to vote somebody out of show business."

—Steve Martin, hosting the 73rd Annual Academy Awards

Name That Dialogue

There's a high-tech version of this game that involves gathering all the movie DVDs, finding lines that aren't obscured by music or sound effects, recording them onto a CD and then...ugh. I'm sorry, but just thinking about it makes me tired. If you want to do all that, knock yourself out. On the other hand, the low-tech version involves nothing more complicated than paper. I recommend that for the following reasons:

If you go high-tech, your guests will only sit
still for about 20 pieces of dialogue, but the
low-tech version will keep them occupied
for as many as 30 or so.

You don't have to search for lines of dialogue
"in the clear." If you want to use the line, "I'll
never let go!" you can do it without worrying if the sound of the Titanic upending
and sinking into the icy Atlantic along with
1,500 screaming CGI passengers is going to
drown it out.

You don't have to bring the room to a screech-
ing halt to play the game, forcing everyone to
listen to some cockamamie CD you created.

Since it's on paper, you can hand it out as
people come in, admonishing them with a
sly wink not to cheat. And of course they'll
cheat but who cares. This is an Oscar party,
not the Citadel.

To create this competition on paper, select the lines you want to use. Be sure to include some from this year's Academy Award nominees. Then go for the usual easily guessed lines so that even your stupidest guests can get some right. Add some obscure pieces, too—so the hard-core movie buffs can feel smug about getting them—and a couple from movies that only you and your best pal saw so you can give your friend an unfair advantage.

Once you've selected the quotes, print out a page with the quote and a blank line where your contestants write in the title of the movie.

Note: Just because you *think* you know the line doesn't mean you *do*. For instance, at no point in *Casablanca* does anyone actually say, "Play it again, Sam." And in #1 above, most people imitating Scarlett's histrionics usually say, "I'll never *go* hungry again" when in fact it's "...*be* hungry...." Do your research.

Grading the Results

1. When you decide it's time to see who won, get everyone's attention.
2. Have everyone exchange the papers they wrote their answers on (so nobody is "grading" their own).
3. You announce the correct answers while your guests mark the papers. The person who wrote down the most correct answers wins.
4. If there's a tie, refer to Chapter Twelve, which

is conveniently filled with tiebreaker questions for that very purpose.

5. With great style and flair, dole out the prize(s).

Really Getting into It

I have been to Oscar parties where the host was a manic-obsessive, balls-out, thermonuclear movie freak. If that describes you, hooray!—and I'm busy Oscar night. But for those of you who really, *really* like getting into the how-well-do-you-know-your-movies   competitions, you're going to love editing together a couple of these competitions for your party.

Now, if you just went, "Me? *Editing* something together? No way, Oprah's on," then stick with the competitions I described earlier. For you, anything that sounds like work is *not* something you're inclined to enjoy, and who can blame you? As far as I'm concerned, work is why God made other people and a service economy. But for those of you to whom this sounds like more fun than Gay Day at Disney World, and who jump at the chance to show off your technical expertise, extensive DVD/soundtrack collection, and pointlessly profound knowledge of movies, this Bud's for you.

Besides, as any geek will tell you, if a person has the motivation and the right equipment, editing is easy. In this digital age where almost everything is readily available on DVD, CD, or mp3, putting together these competitions is a snap. With technology at our sticky fingertips, we're easily able to edit together the bits of dialogue, music, or movies to create these contests. Competitions like:

Name That Picture

The purely visual aspect of movies is what burns them into our memories. The snow globe in *Citizen Kane,* the pristine desert of *Lawrence of Arabia*, Divine eating dog shit in *Pink Flamingos*, it all has been seared into our collective cortex for good or ill. And that's why we want to make a game of it.

For the purposes of this game I assume two things. One, you own or have access to a myriad of movies on DVD. And two, you have the time to invest, because it entails at least doing chapter searches on each movie to get the scene you want to edit onto the DVD you're making for this competition.

Stack the DVDs of the movies you love the most near your computer. Go through them to find the scenes you wish to record. If it's a well-known film, you might select one of the lesser scenes from it just to make that one more challenging to identify. Or you might want to select an iconic scene, such as Jack Twist and Ennis Del Mar kissing after being apart for years or Vivien Bell and Cay Rivvers finally getting it on.

Spark up the competition by juxtaposing your scenes, just like a film editor. For instance, the scene from *The Birds* where the birds are attacking the schoolchildren running down the street can be placed right before the scene in *High Anxiety* where, in a famous takeoff, Mel Brooks is fleeing birds that are massively crapping on him. Or the scene in *Jaws* where the huge shark surfaces in front of Roy Scheider, leading him to say, "You're gonna need a bigger boat," can be edited right before a long-shot of the much bigger boat in *Titanic* for comic effect. Play. Have fun. Enjoy.

You might also consider going with a theme, such as:

- Naked and/or topless women—a big hit with the lezzies
- Naked and/or topless men—a way to entice the guys to participate
- Famous butts of Hollywood (all can enjoy, plus a parade of asses is always funny)
- Gay-themed movies
- Homoerotic scenes (not necessarily gay— think westerns, military, pirate, etc.)

Each scene should be about 15 to 30 seconds long so that your guests will have time to identify the movie and write down the title. Keep the total number of scenes to around 15 so that interest doesn't have a chance to wane.

OK, so you've assembled your scenes and burned them to a DVD. Now you need to create the sheet your guests will use to write down the movie titles. It should look pretty much like this:

Movie #1: _____

Movie #2: _____

Movie #3: _____

(etc.)

Don't forget to type a "key," too, so that afterward you'll be able to call out the correct answers. *Make sure your key is accurate.* If you get a movie wrong, mix up a couple of titles, or have all the answers one number off, you'll face immediate, scathing, and warranted scorn from your guests. Check your stuff to make sure it's right.

On party night—before the pre-show starts, thank you—hand out the sheets with the numbered blanks you created per the directions above, along with writing implements.

Get the attention of your guests and explain that they are to write down the name of the movie each scene is from. When they're ready, grab your remote and start playing your impeccably produced DVD of movie scenes.

To be sure that everyone knows which scene they're watching and which blank on the sheet to fill in, call out, "Movie #1," "Movie #2," etc. That way, a person who can't think of the movie title for the scene they're watching knows when to give up and move on to the next.

When you've finished the DVD, instruct your guests to exchange their sheets with someone else, so nobody is "grading" their own. Using your "key," announce the correct answers while the guests mark the papers. The person with the most correct answers wins. If there's a tie, well, that's what all those lists in Chapter Twelve are for. Hand out the prize(s) with great fanfare.

Name That Score

The Name That Picture competition was visual, while this one is purely aural. Edit together brief sections of music from movies, and have your guests try to identify the films they're from.

Pick a section of the soundtrack that contains a line of the melody—enough for a person who knows the music to be able to recognize it. Then move on to the next. Edit artfully so it's doesn't sound like you didn't care how you chopped it. You may decide to put a short tone between each selection to indicate the transition, or perhaps a fade-out will do. If you're anal, feel free to splice in "Cut #1," "Cut #2," etc., as you go.

Don't get carried away—musical phrases from 10 to 15 films are as many as any group will stand—er sit still—for. And this is also enough to include this year's Academy Award nominees, plus your favorites, a bunch of "gimmes," and some obscure pieces. Once you have it assembled, burn a CD of it.

Make a "key" to track which cut is from which movie. Check and double-check to make sure you've got the correct answer to each cut so an angry music fan doesn't get pissed off and pour Drano in your koi pond.

At your party, give each player a photocopied piece of paper that looks something like this:

Cut #1: _____

Cut #2: _____

Cut #3: _____

(etc.)

And so on for as many cuts of music as you have. Play the CD. Guests must identify the movie next to the number of the cut played. When you get to the end of your edited pieces, have everyone exchange the papers. Announce the correct answers. You guessed it—the person who wrote down the most correct answers wins. If there's a tie, go to the tiebreaker questions in Chapter Twelve. Award the prize(s) with pomp and circumstance.

Yes Award/ No Award: Directors

There are great directors the Academy has honored as well as overlooked. Sometimes, if it becomes glaringly obvious, the Academy will try to make up for the oversight with an honorary award. But that's not what this quiz is about. And many directors have been nominated in other categories such as Best Screenplay or Best Visual Effects, but, again, that ain't what we're going for here. Try to guess which of these directors have won Academy Awards *for directing* and which has not.

> *D. W. Griffith*
> *Victor Fleming*
> *James Ivory*
> *George Lucas*
> *John Ford*
> *Otto Preminger*
> *Elia Kazan*
> *Lina Wertmüller*
> *Martin Scorsese*
> *Ron Howard*

Yes Award/ No Award: Directors

Stanley Kubrick

Fritz Lang

Spike Lee

Vincente Minnelli

Jane Campion

David Lean

Woody Allen

Federico Fellini

Cecil B. DeMille

Alfred Hitchcock

Frank Capra

Sofia Coppola

Billy Wilder

Sam Mendes

CHAPTER NINE

Prepping for Your Party

"Oh, my God, I got here! I cannot tell you what I have been through, getting ready for this star-studded event! I had my hair tortured by Emilio! I had my body pummeled by Ambrosia! I had my nails filed by Philippe! I have been worked over by more aliens than Sigourney Weaver! Oh, my God, but I *made* it!"

—Bette Midler, presenting at the 59th Annual Academy Awards, and looking *fabulous*

Time Line

To accomplish anything, you need a proper countdown. It's the only way to have all the elements in place in time for the Oscar telecast. I mean, if you've decided you simply *have* to have homemade kimchee on the menu in honor of the Best Foreign Film nominee from Korea, you'd better have your cabbage chopped and a hole dug in your yard a week prior or you're screwed.

If you've ordered decorations or furniture online, you need to know how long it's going to take to get from Hollywood—or wherever—to you. If you've calculated properly, they'll arrive in time and you won't be reduced to torching your apartment in desperation so you can tell people you selected a "Burning of Atlanta" theme for your party.

Even the Academy has a well-established time line for getting the Oscar show up and running. Theirs runs like this:

- December 1: The deadline for official screen-credit forms to qualify films for consideration.
- December 31: The awards season ends at midnight. (Oh, how dramatic!)
- January 13 or so: The deadline for the nomination ballots.
- January 23 or so: The nominations are announced at the ungodly hour of 5:30 a.m. (Pacific time) in the Samuel Goldwyn Theater in the Academy of Motion Picture

Arts and Sciences building in Beverly Hills.

- February 7 or so: The final ballots are mailed to voters.
- February 20 or so: The deadline for the final ballots.
- February 25 or so: It's Oscar time! The official telecast happens and your guests will be comparing every Oscar party they've ever attended to the one you're throwing that night.

Your time line might look something like this:

- December 1: Put up your Christmas tree. The Oscars are so far from your mind that you give them only a fleeting thought as you hang your Christopher Radko/Dorothy Gale decoration front and center.
- December 31: See at least three of the "important" movies released this week in time to meet Oscar's deadline. Sneak from one theater to the other during the holiday rush, saving your money for something important, like Red Vines.
- January 13 or so: Decide you'll have an Oscar Party. Roll back over, continue nap.
- January 23 or so: Notice that the nominations have been announced. As you peruse them, you think (a) "Is everybody in Hollywood on crack?" and (b) "If I'm going to have a party, I've got to get my ass in gear!" Start by asking people for donations for your swag bags.

- February 7 or so: The final invitations are mailed. Get the stuff you need to purchase for the swag bags and prizes.
- February 20 or so: The final RSVPs are in. Make sure the menu is settled, and the decorations are on their way. Shop for prizes and whatnot.
- Day before the Oscars: Take down that freaking Christmas tree!
- February 25 or so: It's Oscar night—and your guests will be having a much better time at your party than those Hollywood phonies at theirs!

OK, so it may not run exactly like that, but you get the idea. Like they say in Weight Watchers—or is that in 12-Step?—"If you fail to plan, you plan to fail."

Your To-Do List

This is vital, boys and girls. You'll need a pad and pencil, a calendar, and a good idea of what you want your party to look like and what you want to do during it.

Make a list of what you want to have at your Oscar Party.

Write down what you need to do to accomplish those things.

Shopping
Ordering
Cooking
Building and creating

Asking friends and businesses for swag and
   other donations
Assembling
Mailing
Renting and borrowing
Putting together the balloting and other games
   and activities
Picking up the items ordered, rented, borrowed,
   etc

Get a calendar. Make sure it has plenty of space to write on per day.

Mark the date of the Academy Awards, the date of your Oscar Party.

Working backward, establish due dates for everything on your list. Make sure to give yourself ample leeway in case something arrives late or you get in a time crunch.

Post this calendar with all your due dates by the phone or, if you're like me, on the fridge, where I spend the majority of my time.

Stick to the dates and deadlines you've made for yourself! If you get behind, you'll have the devil's own time catching up, so don't allow yourself to do that.

Get two separate sheets of paper. On the top of one write "Saturday," and on the other write "Sunday." These are for the day before and day of your party. Write down the hours of the day on each sheet. Now, just as you did with the days of the month on the calendar, work backward listing everything you need to have in your house, on the walls, in the fridge, on the table, set up for display, ready for use, and otherwise on hand. Don't forget to include time to get yourself bathed, plucked, powdered, and presentable (more on that in Chapter Nine). Again, *give yourself ample time for these tasks.* That way, you won't be a frenzied, frazzled mess by the time the guests arrive.

If you follow this plan, you'll have time to accomplish your décor, assemble your prizes and swag, prepare your party games, set out refreshments, dress, and center yourself with a deep, cleansing breath and a Long Island iced tea. You'll be ready to greet your guests in gracious style and get the evening's events underway with a minimum of stress—because you planned, you prepared, and you stuck to your time line!

Honey, You Need Help!

Feeling overwhelmed? It's not surprising. Just look at all you have to do on the evening of your party:

Greet guests.

Hand out and explain ballots.

Keep food table stocked.

See to the beverages.

Make sure there's always ice.

Oversee the ballot tallies.

Distribute swag bags.

Run contests and competitions.

Provide tie-breaking questions if needed.

Hand out awards and prizes.

Keep the party "happening."

Pick up trash.

Take out trash.

Check bathroom(s).

which movie will recieve most awards

You can either kill yourself doing everything all by your lonesome, or do what I heartily recommend: Enlist your friends and family in helping. One can be Kitchen Kommandant, one Viewing Area Vixen, etc., each responsible for keeping their purview maintained, relatively tidy, and, most important, festive. This will free you up to be the star.

Dole out the duties that you don't want. Just be sure you can trust them to follow through. It's awfully easy to get so caught up in the drama of whether the Best Supporting Actress winner will be able to finish her blithering acceptance speech before the orchestra cuts her off that your friend Tré neglects to watch the rumaki he was assigned to warm in the oven and you end up with bacon-wrapped anthracite. Pick people who can focus.

After the party, you need to have something special for your little helpers. After all, they sacrificed the pure Oscar party experience so you could shine in all your tawdry wannabe glory. Cash may be considered by some to be crass, but if the truth were told, your friends would rather have that than some token of your well-intended if errant esteem such as the boxed set of *Xena Warrior Princess,* Seasons 1–3. So split the difference and get each helper a $20 to $25 gift certificate card to a place they frequently visit. I love gift cards. It's a gesture that says, "Obligation met."

Hired Hands

Depending on the scale of your Oscar party—and whether or not you have any friends—consider hiring someone to do some of the work. It makes no sense to run yourself ragged trying to do everything, especially since that tends to make a body stressed out and cranky and that's no party for anyone. Think about it: Are you going to be so busy that you can't enjoy your own party?

In some situations, even friends aren't going to be able to help you out like you need. Becky may be the greatest car mechanic in the world, but she may suck at mixing a drink and keeping the crudités coming. If you hire someone for this, it'll free up Becky to join your party (and not screw up your drinks). You'll get an experienced caterer whom you can yell at without worrying they know how to tamper with your brakes.

Another great reason to hire people is that—within some bounds of reason—you can make them do pretty much anything. If your theme is *Planet of the Apes* and you want 'em to wear a gorilla mask…guess what? They gotta.

And don't forget the possibility of hiring specialty help. Want your bartender (and anyone else you hire) to be big, buff, and basically bare? Explain to the agency that your party theme is *Muscle Beach Party* and you expect your employees to be OK with serving homos in Speedos. If they don't hang up on you, that's who they'll send. For those so inclined, if you want big, *bosomy*, and basically bare, do the same thing only tell them the theme is *Baywatch* or even *Showgirls*.

When the evening is over and the gorilla heads come off, *tip your hired help* $20 to $25 apiece. More if you made them prance in their skivvies, serve in drag, or wear something offensive, repugnant, and demeaning like a Republican president mask.

Since you'll have to shell out for these folks, keep their

cost in mind when you make your party list. Remember your party list back in Chapter Two? No? *Somebody* needs to look back and review!

"I'm Running Out of Time!"

A word about budgeting. Time is a budget item, too. You only have so much of it, and when it's gone, that's it, girlfriend. That's why you made your time line and your to-do list. And even then, shit happens.

Count on something unexpected coming up to throw off your schedule utterly. Your ex comes for a visit; Spot eats a dozen dental dams; Cher comes through with yet another farewell tour. These things are bigger than you, beyond your control, and must be dealt with. Or maybe you're just a lazy-ass wasting your days eating Cheetos and watching Nickelodeon. Either way, it's going to eat into your party planning time. That means you will be forced into making decisions about which aspect(s) of your soiree to eliminate. Keep that in mind as your deadline—Oscar day—approaches.

Prioritize!

As your deadline looms, always have a little list going in the back of your mind of what you could do *without*. Prioritize! Know what is more—and less—important to carry off the evening you have planned. As crunch time approaches, be prepared to *cut some less important items.*

I can't stress enough the importance of being flexible with your plans. Remember, the point of all this is to provide a good time for your friends *as well as yourself.*

If you're a nervous, wornout wreck, not only will you be miserable but your guests will be affected by that. In order for you to have a sane and enjoyable time, if it becomes necessary to forgo the decorations or the Name the Movie competition or the six-course meal, *let it go!*

If you're still uncomfortable with the idea of cutting back on your festivities, remember this about your guests: *They won't know what they didn't get.* They'll be thrilled with whatever you do provide, say, Chinese takeout, and they won't have a clue that you'd originally intended to redo the entire house in *Crouching Tiger, Hidden Dragon* décor.

Your Oscar-Party Planner

This is not meant to be a list of everything you *must* have to have a successful party. This is a checklist to help *you* decide what you want to have, and to help you assemble it for your fabulous do. It's also possible to use this list to help you decide what you can do *without*. Use it however it serves you best.

Invitations:

___ By mail
___ By telephone
___ By email
___ By mouth
___ RSVP cutoff date

The Room:

___ In your home
___ At another location?
___ Cleaned

___ Theme chosen
___ Caterer (that could be you, your friends, or hired workers)
___ Liquor
___ Wine
___ Bartender(s)
___ Beverages
___ Ice
___ Appetizers/crudités/hors d'oeuvres
___ Printed list(s) of "house rules"
___ Display of charity you're fundraising for

Décor:

___ Items you have
___ Items you can borrow
___ Items rented or purchased
___ Furniture
___ Walls
___ Ceiling treatment(s)
___ Flowers
___ Balloons
___ Glitter
___ Confetti

Food Area:

___ Make food list
___ Purchase food
___ Timetable for preparing food
___ Prepare food
___ System for warming items
___ System for chilling items
___ Buffet

___ Buffet signage (labeling dishes)
___ Work out logistics of serving
___ Plates
___ Cups/glasses
___ Cutlery
___ Napkins
___ Trash
___ System for taking care of the trash

Swag Bags:

___ The bags themselves
___ Donated swag
___ Purchased swag
___ Assemble swag in bags
___ Storage for swag bags until end of telecast/ party

Competition(s):

___ Ballots
___ Pens/pencils
___ Printed and copied sheets for competitions
___ Edited CD(s)
___ Edited DVD(s)
___ Paper slips with movie titles for charades
___ Script(s) for Oscar-winning performance game
___ Prizes and awards for each competition

Q List #4:
"Special" Awards for
"Special" People

From time to time the Academy will trot out someone they deem "special" and shove a Jean Hersholt Humanitarian Award or Irving G. Thalberg Memorial Award at them. For years you've probably thought, "Who the hell are these guys," followed quickly by, "Who cares—I'm going to freshen my drink." Well, while you're attending to your adult beverage, let me educate you.

The Jean Hersholt Humanitarian Award

This award is not only a high honor because it's not competitive, it can be also be the dullest part of any Academy Awards show not hosted by David Letterman. Fortunately it's only awarded periodically. It's named after screen actor Jean Hersholt (*Dinner at Eight*, *Heidi*, *Grand Hotel*), who was president of the Motion Picture Relief Fund for 18 years. (Now the Motion Picture and Television Fund, this organization provides health plans, hospital services, and a retirement community to those working in the entertainment industry.)

The trophy is an Oscar statuette and the people who have won it are all over the map: producers, directors, writers, and actors. Officially it's given out for outstanding contributions to humanitarian causes, but by and large it's *really* given out to people the Academy likes and who they know are never going to get an Oscar. And why shouldn't the Academy do that? It's their party. Unfortunately, handing it out puts a damper on *our* party. So we're going to turn this turkey into a…game! For example, ask your guests what homosexual won the Hersholt in 1981. Whoever gets it, reward them generously. After all, this is a freaking humanitarian award!

The recipients for the years it was presented are:
1956 Y. Frank Freeman
1957 Samuel Goldwyn
1959 Bob Hope
1960 Sol Lesser
1961 George Seaton
1962 Steve Broidy
1965 Edmond L. DePatie
1966 George Bagnall
1967 Gregory Peck
1968 Martha Raye
1969 George Jessel
1970 Frank Sinatra
1972 Rosalind Russell
1973 Lew Wasserman
1974 Arthur B. Krim
1975 Dr. Jules C. Stein
1977 Charlton Heston
1978 Leo Jaffe
1979 Robert Benjamin
1981 Danny Kaye
1982 Walter Mirisch
1983 M. J. Frankovich
1984 David L. Wolper

1985 Charles "Buddy" Rogers
1989 Howard W. Koch
1992 Audrey Hepburn, Elizabeth Taylor
1993 Paul Newman
1994 Quincy Jones
2001 Arthur Hiller
2005 Roger Mayer

The Irving G. Thalberg Memorial Award

Irving Thalberg became head of production at the Universal Film Manufacturing Co. at the age of 20. (Uh-huh. And what were *you* doing at 20?) Three years later he was made vice president and head of production for Louis B. Mayer. The next year, when Mayer's studio became part of Metro-Goldwyn-Mayer (MGM), Thalberg was made vice president and supervisor of production and for the next eight years MGM was Hollywood's most prestigious studio, with Thalberg himself supervising (almost always uncredited) the studio's top productions. We're talking movies like *The Good Earth, Camille, Romeo and Juliet, Mutiny on the Bounty,* and the Marx Brothers' classics *A Day at the Races* and *A Night at the Opera.* In 1936 the poor bastard died of pneumonia at the age of 37. The following year the Academy instituted the Irving G. Thalberg Memorial Award. It's not an Oscar statuette, but a solid bronze head of Thalberg on a base of black marble base. It weighs 10¾ pounds and is nine inches tall. Mercifully it's not given out every year, either, but like the Hersholt Award, only when the board feels it is merited.

Officially it's presented to "creative producers whose bodies of work reflect a consistently high quality of motion picture production." But looking at the list (below), you can see it's given out to the really talented folks Oscar basically overlooked. With admitted exceptions, it's a kind of "make up" award. So feel free to "make up" questions to regale and challenge your guests.

The recipients for the years it was presented are:
1937 Darryl F. Zanuck
1938 Hal B. Wallis
1939 David O. Selznick
1941 Walt Disney
1942 Sidney Franklin
1943 Hal B. Wallis
1944 Darryl F. Zanuck
1946 Samuel Goldwyn
1948 Jerry Wald
1950 Darryl F. Zanuck
1951 Arthur Freed
1952 Cecil B. DeMille
1953 George Stevens
1956 Buddy Adler
1958 Jack L. Warner
1961 Stanley Kramer
1963 Sam Spiegel
1965 William Wyler
1966 Robert Wise
1967 Alfred Hitchcock
1970 Ingmar Bergman
1973 Lawrence Weingarten
1975 Mervyn LeRoy

1976 Pandro S. Berman
1977 Walter Mirisch
1979 Ray Stark
1981 Albert R. Broccoli
1986 Steven Spielberg
1987 Billy Wilder
1990 David Brown and Richard D. Zanuck
1991 George Lucas
1994 Clint Eastwood
1996 Saul Zaentz
1998 Norman Jewison
1999 Warren Beatty
2000 Dino De Laurentiis

CHAPTER TEN

Oscar Night: The Pre-Show

[*Singing:*] "It's a wonderful night for Oscar! Oscar, Oscar! Who will win?"

—Billy Crystal, hosting the 62nd Annual Academy Awards

YOU, BEING the fabulous Hollywood hostess that you are, care desperately about everything Tinseltown, so you already had the TV on when the first limos started arriving shortly after lunch. You are there for the glamour, the glitz, the gowns. You are there to see whom Joan Rivers and her forgettable daughter malign and misidentify, whom Mizrahi is going to poke and grope—and why God created the E! network.

As you watch the pre-show, taking in all the inane, unbelievably stupid things people say, do, and wear, you and your guests will be unable to refrain from sharing cruel, cutting, and hilarious comments. It's one of the reasons gay and lesbian people are on the planet. We are the children pointing at the emperor and declaring that, despite the Giambattista Valli gown and Harry Winston jewels, "These A-holes have no clothes!" Yes, my sisters, it has fallen to us to remind each other, if not the world, that these glamorous millionaires deserve to be taken down a peg or five because, for all their posturing, they sweat, burp, fart, piss, poop, and do the nasty just like everyone else.

It's just too much damn fun to take well-aimed potshots at the pompous. In fact, all this is just a lead-up to telling you how we're going to make a competition out of it!

The Bitch Queen: The *All-Night* Competition!

"This is the night that Hollywood puts aside its petty jealousies and brings out its major jealousies."

—Johnny Carson, hosting of the 54th Annual Academy Awards

For the pre-show you must, simply *must*, have a totem that represents the Bitch Queen. Whether it's Joan Rivers's head pasted on cardboard and taped to a broom handle or the image of the Red Queen really doesn't matter so long as you have something recognizable and wieldy enough to be able to pass.

And here is how you use it.

Guests are assembled for television pre-show viewing an hour before the show starts. With great fanfare, present the Bitch Queen totem and explain its function, which is this: Whoever makes the best, wickedest, funniest, and frankest comment gets the honor of holding the totem. The decision is in the hands of the other guests, so everyone is involved. When someone delivers an evil but hilarious bon mot about the people, clothes, or general proceedings on television, it is the decision of the group as to whether the Bitch Queen totem should now move to that person. Generally this can be perceived by the majority of the guests within earshot going, "*Oooh!*" in jealous appreciation. When that happens, the totem moves to that person and remains there until someone else comes up with something even more snarky and fun. Whoever holds the totem is responsible for defending it, too. He or she must continue to top whatever comments others are tossing at the screen. When that person is bested, the totem moves on. Be gracious about giving it up.

This continues for the duration of the evening, even as the other activities such as drinking games, balloting, etc., are going on. You want an interesting mix of stuff happening all during the night. That way, if the awards become predictable and the balloting gets dull, you still have this fun activity working in the background. The Bitch Queen competition creates the always-lurking incentive for someone to liven things up by shouting out something cruel, inappropriate, and, most important, hysterical.

"You were very good playing a bitch-heroine, but you shouldn't win an award for playing yourself."

—Jack Warner to Bette Davis after she failed to win an Oscar as Best Actress for *Of Human Bondage* (1935)

Bitch Queen Rules

Be very explicit about pointing out the only three rules for this competition:

1. The decision of the group is *final*.
2. The person holding the totem at the time the group reacts positively to another person's zinger *must pass it on* with goodwill and generosity.
3. Most important, *all derogatory comments must be aimed at the people on TV, not at the people in the room.*

After all, you want everyone at your party to have a good time and watch the Oscars. If one guest jumps into another's business about something that causes an ugly scene, it will distract from the general enjoyment of the evening. Worse, it will have an unfortunate tendency to focus attention away from the party you laid out far too much money for. No, no. The barbs are directed only at the stars, not at the guests.

Whoever is holding the totem at the conclusion of the Oscar telecast is proclaimed the Bitch Queen. Have a prize on hand. A simple, tasteful appropriately bitchy DVD will do fine. May I suggest:

- *Mommie Dearest*
- *Mean Girls*
- *Heathers* (or pretty much anything with Shannon Doherty)
- *Whatever Happened to Baby Jane?*
- *Saved* (keep Mandy Moore's Hillary Fay in mind for your totem topper)
- *Mother's Boys* (Jamie Lee Curtis in a role that'd scare Michael Myers)
- *Who's Afraid of Virginia Woolf?* (Oscar-winning bitches in this one!)
- Any Disney flick with a cool evil villain: Scar, Ursula, Cruella De Vil, etc.

OK, Maybe Not "Bitch Queen"

If the term "bitch" offends you, keep in mind that in gay vocabulary it can be an endearment. Gaia certainly knows women have been put down more than enough by straight men as well as by some unenlightened gay men. But there are two very important things you need to remember.

First, the Bitch Queen is merely an archetype. She

represents the dark side of the very powerful Mother archetype, embodying the great energy of the good-mother-gone-awry. Instead of the positive nurturing aspect of the feminine, it is the smothering, self-centered, I-will-bring-you-down side. It may not be what you hope for in your own mother, but it sure does make for all the best drama—not to mention high-quality catty comments in which we all love to indulge. So whichever side emerges from this Mother archetype, dark or light, it's that expression of the feminine that carries such enormous psychic power for us queers. As any drag performer can tell you, this metaphoric sexuality is embraced for its power (whether you're a good witch or a bad witch), not for denigration of the feminine. Got that? Thank God. Now we can move on. (Plus, you just earned a credit in Anthropological Archetypes from your local community college.) Besides, what else would you call Ted Casablanca if not Bitch Queen?

And the second thing you should remember if you're offended and don't like the party totem being called the Bitch Queen: You can *make it something else!* Make it a man, a non-gender-specific animal, a sexually neutral object like a pillow for Goddess' sake. Darling, this is *your party,* not mine. You have the power to do or not do anything in this book.

That said, I'm still going to give you some ideas for whose head you can jam on the end of a stick for your totem:

Prime Hollywood Bitches

Ted Casablanca
Joan Rivers

Isaac Mizrahi

Paris Hilton

Martha (I know, I love her, too, but we've all
heard the tales)

Simon Cowell

Miss Piggy

Madonna (it's a power thing, remember)

Barbra (ditto, girlfriend!)

That hard-ass lesbian down the street

That bitter hair-burner who can't keep a
boyfriend and won't shut up about it

Q Facts #2: Random Fun Backstage Stuff

At the first Academy Awards ceremony, which took place in the Blossom Room of the Hollywood Roosevelt Hotel on May 16, 1929, a dinner for the 270 Academy members and guests was served. On the menu:

- Consommé
- Filet of sole
- Broiled chicken
- Potatoes
- String beans

And on each table were waxed candy replicas of the Oscar statuette.

Me-ow!

When Bette Davis and Joan Crawford starred together in 1962's *Whatever Happened to Baby Jane?* only Bette got a Best Actress nomination. Joan was so pissed off by the snub that she wrote letters to the other four nominees, congratulating them and offering to accept their awards if they couldn't make it to the show. That year Anne Bancroft won, and, yes, Joan accepted it on her behalf. Bette could only stand by fuming. Love that!

And the Winner Is…

In Oscar's early days and throughout the 1930s, the newspapers were given advance notification of the winners so they could publish the results the night of the ceremony. In 1937 Best Actress nominee Gladys George took advantage of this to leave her seat and stroll through the press room, where she unhappily learned she'd lost to Luise Rainer. Later George ran into odds-on favorite Carole Lombard in the powder room. Naturally George couldn't resist telling Lombard that she, too, was a loser. All around it just wasn't a pretty night.

Three years later, after some of the guests and nominees bought the late edition of the *Los Angeles Times* to read the results *on their way to the Oscar ceremony,* the Academy decided to go with the now-famous sealed envelopes and extreme secrecy.

And Stay Out!

In 1982 Zbigniew Rybczynski won for Best Animated Short Oscar as producer of *Tango*. He stepped outside for a cigarette. When he tried to get back into the Dorothy Chandler Pavilion, the security guard refused to readmit the Polish filmmaker. Rybczynski pleaded, "I have Oscar!" but to no avail. Totally pissed off, Rybczynski kicked the guard and was promptly arrested and thrown in jail. When will people understand that *nobody* is allowed to smoke in LA!

First Elijah Wood Sighting

Elijah Wood made his first appearance at the Oscar telecast at the age of 13, eight years before appearing as Frodo Baggins in *The Lord of the Rings*. He handed out the award for Best Visual Effects, but there's more to this story. Originally Macaulay Culkin had been booked to present that award, but young Master Culkin didn't like the script and insisted his lines be rewritten. *Some*body's head swelled after a couple of *Home Alone*s, huh? Oh, wouldn't you have loved to have been at that rehearsal to see his hairless ass get fired for being a diva and then get replaced by his *Good Son* costar, Elijah Wood! Good times!

CHAPTER ELEVEN

Adapting These Preparations to Other Award Shows

QUOTE

"I'm thinking about naming my first son Emmy so I can say I've got one. I want Emmy, Oscar and Tony— and my daughter Grammy."

—Noah Wyle

IF YOU want to celebrate awards shows like the Golden Globes, the Daytime Emmys, or any of those other events where Hollywood industry folks manage to pat their own backs while simultaneously autofellating (not that the Academy does that or anything), I'm happy to help. If, however, you're only here for the Oscar awards (and who could blame you?), skip ahead to the next chapter full of tiebreaker questions. Go on. Go.

You're staying? Very well, then, read on.

Parties for Other Awards Shows: An Overview

As Gertrude Stein would have said had she sat down to write this chapter, "A party is a party is a party." Certain elements are common to all parties. The invitations, preparations, and festive-atmosphere creation are to be had at any halfway decent soiree. And never underestimate the effects of alcohol, both good and bad. Like it or not, because we are gay and lesbian, there's a certain expectation put upon us by the rest of the world that our parties should be that "little extra something" better and have that *je ne c'est quois* so frequently absent at other parties (unless the host was wise enough to have it planned and catered by us).

So as we look to creating a party for, say, the Tony Awards, we'll carry over many of the highly festive elements discussed in the previous Oscar-oriented pages. Your task—and it is a simple one—will be to take those elements and adapt them to the specific awards at hand.

Things that are for all awards:

- The mechanics of the actual party planning (see Chapter One)
- Naming your food and drinks after the nominated shows, movies, artists, etc. (see Chapter Four)
- Trophies, posters, and tchotchkes as prizes and giveaways (Ssee Chapter Five)

- Various samples, coupons, candies and party-store items for swag bags (also Chapter Five)
- Charades and the Drinking Game (see Chapter Eight)
- Getting help if you need it (see Chapter Nine)
- The Bitch-Queen Game (see Chapter Ten)

> "Even if I hadn't have been nominated for an Oscar, to have won the Golden Glove [sic] was just fantastic."
>
> —Brenda Blethyn in 1997 after winning the "Golden Glove" for Best Actress for *Secrets and Lies*

The Golden Globes

THEME: The Globes, put on by the Hollywood Foreign Press Association, include both movies and television categories, so that expands the possibilities for your theme considerably. Look at the movies and see what suggests itself to you. Don't like 'em? Then look at the TV shows up for awards. Or go for classic TV shows.

FOOD AND DRINK: The folks at the Golden Globes are all sitting at tables eating dinner and drinking. I suggest you do the same while watching. It'll help you feel like you and your guests are a part of the occasion. The more you can make it look like hotel-ballroom dining, the better. If that means paper plates and plastic wine glasses on TV trays, go with it. After all, you don't have the hotel staff to clean up for you.

BALLOTING: God bless the foreigners! Even as the Hollywood Foreign Press Association considers itself artistically superior, it's consistently overcome by the unabashed, loveable, whiz-bang pop culture we Americans pump out like bilge after a Carnival Cruise. The result is a mixed bag of outright worshipping of crap, tempered with artsy-fartsy choices here and there. Good luck predicting that. To get the ballot supplied by the Hollywood Foreign Press Association go to www.hfpa.org. Follow the scoring of your guests' ballots as described for the Oscars in Chapter Six.

The Primetime Emmys

THEME: Pick your favorite TV show up for an award. Or go with a classic.

FOOD AND DRINK: Are you kidding? TV dinners are the only possibility. Augment with TV-watching snack foods like chips (potato and tortilla), dips, nuts, and cheese.

BALLOTING: Go to www.emmys.org and click on link for the Annual Primetime Emmy Awards. Follow the scoring of your guests' ballots as described for the Oscars in Chapter Six.

The Daytime Emmys

THEME: I know these awards encompass talk shows, game shows, and all kinds of other stuff, but it's the daytime soap operas that rule. I suggest you and your guests all overdress in trampy/studly clothes. Then spend the entire time relating to each other archly, as if you had more dirt on the other person than Erika Kane had on all of Pine Valley. Sharpen your claws and let your inner diva out. It's role-playing heaven. You'll love it.

FOOD AND DRINK: Cheese! Don't get me wrong. I love my soaps, but if the daytime dramas aren't all about cheese I don't know what is. Possible menu:

ALL MY CHILDREN CHILI
   Like Sandwiches Through the Hourglass ham
      (for the acting) with American cheese (for
      the plots)
   To drink: Port Charles port or Lords of Llan-
      view Llemonade
   And for dessert: *Bold and Beautiful* Bananas
      Forrester

BALLOTING: Go to www.emmys.org, click on the link to Annual Daytime Emmy Awards. Follow the scoring as described for the Oscars in Chapter Six.

> "I've got a checklist of things I want, including a Brit, a Grammy, an Oscar and a white poodle. Sometimes it gets lonely, and I want a baby, too! I'm ticking things off the list."
>
> —Singer Joss Stone, after being nominated for three Grammys in 2005

The Grammys

THEME: This is a gimme—music. Have karaoke before and after the telecast—and maybe even during the longer commercial breaks to make the show more bearable. See if your guests can sing the nominated songs better than the original artists (yeah, right!). Encourage guests to come dressed as over-the-top trashy as the nominees. For décor drop by any garage sale and pick up a pile of old vinyl LPs for, you should pardon the expression, a song. Take them out of the sleeves and tape them to the walls and hang them from the ceiling. Since blank CDs are now so cheap, you can intermingle those with the vinyl records for flash.

FOOD AND DRINK: Whatever your guests can eat that

will not leave the karaoke microphone sticky or greasy when they've sung their number. Think crudités and nuts or items that come with individual toothpicks. If you have larger food, make sure it comes with a fork.

BALLOTING: Go to www.grammy.com. You'll have to search around because they change their website from time to time; when you find the list of nominees, use that to create the ballot for your guests. Follow the scoring as described in Chapter Six.

The Tonys

THEME: Broadway! If you're a gay man and you don't have the original cast albums of this year's Best Musical or Best Revival of a Musical playing when people arrive, hand in your Homo Membership card. (If you're a lesbian or straight, you're much more sensible, so you're allowed to skip that.) Feel free to dole out top hats and canes, feather boas, and other theatrical props to your guests. You might even be inspired to have people come dressed as their favorite stage character. Be prepared to cheer loudly for the homo happenings during the ceremony because, this being a theater crowd, they're a lot more open and out about their same-sex partners and sexuality than the Oscars. These days it's rare to watch a Tony Awards show without seeing somebody smooch their lover and thank their "life partner." Which is yet another reason to dress a bit better than you would for, say, the MTV Vulgarity Awards.

FOOD AND DRINK: Since the Tony Awards are a bit more, well, tony than the other awards, you might consider hors d'oeuvres a smidge more upscale than cocktail wieners and bridge mix. Grocery stores have become so specialized in the last 10 years that you can pretty much find frozen goodies to pop in the oven and then pass around. Look for miniquiches, Swedish meatballs, shrimp wraps, cheese puffs, etc. You'll have to shell out for decent paper or plastic plates, but, hey, this is the Tonys.

BALLOTING: Go to www.tonys.org, click on "Nominees and Awards." Follow the scoring as described in Chapter Six. Go, Cherry Jones and Nathan Lane!

"I love this category: Scoring! Yes, that's right! There is a cheap and vulgar joke to be made for this category, and if I were half as cheap as I look in this dress, I would tell it! But I hardly think that appropriate for an occasion as pompous as this one. So we'll save the cheap shots for the People's Choice Awards."

—Bette Midler, presenting at the 59th Annual Academy Awards

The People's Choice Awards

THEME: If the Tonys are high-falutin', the People's Choice Awards are decidedly low-brow. I mean, come on, the winners are decided by ordinary, middle-American schmoes who thought *Will & Grace* was an accurate depiction of the homosexual lifestyle. Of course, they also thought *Friends* was an accurate depiction of the heterosexual lifestyle, so they're not only ignorant but stupid. While this does make the People's Choice results snob-free, they are also dependably taste-free. At least they have the grace not to list their winners as "*Best* Female Movie Star" but only "*Favorite* Female Movie Star." The People's Choice website has "© Proctor & Gamble, Inc." at the bottom, which suggests these awards exist solely as a means to sell you Vicks, Old Spice, and Tampax. At least they also sell Febreze, which you'll need to get the stink out of your home when the show is over. So for all these reasons, I suggest a trailer-park theme. You'll find that more than covered in Chapter One.

FOOD AND DRINK: Chapter Four will tell you what you need in this department.

BALLOTING: Go to www.pcavote.com, click on "Nominees." Follow the scoring as described in Chapter Six.

QUOTE

"And the nominees for Best Soft Drink Product Placement are…*Star Trek: The Pepsi Generation*, *They Call Me Mr. Pibb*, and *Snow White and the Seven-Ups*."

—Oscar presenter on *Futurama*

OK, OK, so the Academy Awards are all about selling garbage, too. But this is as far as I'm going with the non-Oscars. Other awards shows—such as the Blockbuster Entertainment Awards, Teen Choice Awards, Radio Music Awards (and shouldn't that be just on the radio anyway?), MTV Awards, VH1 "Biggies," and Nickelodeon Kid's Choice Awards (which at least has celebrities getting slimed)—I leave you to celebrate or ignore on your own.

I don't know about you, but after all this, I *really* need to get back to the Oscars!

Q List #5:
Gay Oscar Winners
(and Some Nominees)

EVERYBODY WANTS to know who's gay in Hollywood. However, because most people's paychecks in this town depend on public reputations as credible heterosexuals, the majority of gay/lesbian/bi Hollywood is deeply and firmly in the closet and/or in denial. True, some brave souls are out, but they are few and far between. It's a little easier for nonactors to cop to being homo, and a lot easier for dead people.

Behold the following list of people who are associated with Oscar as well as with same-sex-lovin'. I make no claim that this is a complete list. No doubt there are scores of queer filmmakers, both nominees and winners, who remain below the radar for various reasons. I'm sure you can think of a few glaring examples who are not on this list and are the subject of all kinds of speculation. But this list will get you started.

> "Half of Hollywood is gay—at least the people I run into!"
>
> —Sandra Oh, of *Sideways* and TV's *Grey's Anatomy*

Oh, and just in case you're one of the people listed here who feels they need to take offense and call their lawyer, I got most of this info from the online website Wikipedia, so go after them not me, OK? *I'm* not saying you're gay, but I am saying you're listed there as a famous homo.

- Pedro Almodóvar, who won Best Original Screenplay for *Talk to Her* (2002)
- Cecil Beaton, who won Best Costume Design for *Gigi* (1958) and Best Costume Design (color) and Art Direction (color) for *My Fair Lady* (1964)
- Leonard Bernstein, who was nominated but did not win for Best Original Score for *On the Waterfront* (1954)
- Marlon Brando (bisexual), who, out of seven nominations for Best Actor and one for Best Supporting Actor, won for *On the Waterfront* (1954) and *The Godfather* (1972)

- Montgomery Clift, who was nominated for Best Actor three times and Best Supporting Actor once, but never won
- Bruce Cohen, who won as coproducer of Best Picture *American Beauty* (1999)
- Bill Condon, who won Best Adapted Screenplay for *Gods and Monsters* (1998)
- Noel Coward, who won a special award of merit (not a statuette) for "…his outstanding production achievement in *In Which We Serve*"
- George Cukor, who, out of five nominations for Best Director, won for *My Fair Lady* (1964)
- Marlene Dietrich (bisexual), who was nominated for, but did not win, Best Actress in *Morocco* (1930–31)
- Greta Garbo, who was nominated for Best Actress three times, but did not win. However, in 1954 she was awarded a statuette for "her unforgettable screen performances"
- Janet Gaynor, who won for Best Actress for *Seventh Heaven*, *Street Angel*, and *Sunrise* (all three in 1927–28) at the first Academy Awards. Back then you could win for multiple performances
- John Gielgud, who won Best Supporting Actor for *Arthur* (1981)
- Nigel Hawthorne, who was nominated for, but did not win, Best Actor for *The Madness of King George* (1994)

- Todd Haynes, who was nominated for, but did not win, Best Original Screenplay for *Far From Heaven* (2002)
- Edith Head—are you kidding? Out of 35, yes, 35 nominations for Best Costumes, she won eight. This was back when they gave out separate Oscars for black and white and color films. Edith's Oscars were for:

1. *The Heiress*, black and white (1949)
2. *All About Eve*, black and white (1950)
3. *Samson and Delilah*, color (1950)
4. *A Place in the Sun*, black and white (1951)
5. *Roman Holiday*, black and white (1953)
6. *Sabrina*, black and white (1954)
7. *The Facts of Life*, black and white (1960)
8. *The Sting* (1973)

- William Inge, who won Best Original Screenplay for *Splendor in the Grass* (1961)
- James Ivory, who was nominated for Best Director three times, but has never won
- Dan Jinks, who won as coproducer of Best Picture *American Beauty* (1999)
- Elton John, who won Best Original Song for "Can You Feel the Love Tonight" from *The Lion King* (1994)
- Angelina Jolie (bisexual according to an interview on http://lesbianlife.about.com), who won for Best Supporting Actress for *Girl, Interrupted* (1999)
- Tony Kushner, who was nominated for Best

Original Screenplay for *Munich* (2005), but did not win

- Charles Laughton, who, out of three nominations for Best Actor, won for *The Private Life of Henry VIII* (1932–33)
- John Logan, who has two Best Original Screenplay nominations but no wins
- Ian McKellen who has two nominations, but no wins
- Vincente Minnelli, who won Best Director for *Gigi* (1958)
- Agnes Moorehead, who was nominated for Best Supporting Actress four times, but never won
- Laurence Olivier (bisexual), who, out of 11 nominations, won a special award (statuette) in 1946 for "his outstanding achievement as actor, producer, and director in bringing *Henry V* to the screen," a Best Actor Oscar for *Hamlet* (1948), and in 1978 another honorary statuette for "the full body of his work, for the unique achievements of his entire career, and his lifetime of contribution to the art of film"
- Anthony Perkins, who had one nomination for Best Supporting Actor but didn't win
- Cole Porter, who had four nominations for Best Original Song, but didn't win. No wins! *Cole Porter!?!* This is proof Hollywood takes too many drugs
- Jerome Robbins, who won a shared (with Robert Wise, who is straight) Best Direc-

tor Oscar for *West Side Story* (1961), plus another statuette the same year for "his brilliant achievements in the art of choreography on film"

- John Schlesinger, who, out of three nominations for Best Director, won for *Midnight Cowboy* (1969)
- Stephen Sondheim, who won Best Original Song for "Sooner or Later" (sung by Madonna, no less) in *Dick Tracy* (1990)
- Gus Van Sant, who has one nomination for Best Director for *Good Will Hunting* (1997) but didn't win
- Lily Tomlin, who has one nomination for Best Supporting Actress, but didn't win
- Tennessee Williams, who had two nominations for writing, but no wins
- Paul Winfield, who has one nomination for Best Actor, but no wins
- Franco Zeffirelli, who has two nominations, but no wins
- Barbara Stanwyck, who has four best actress nominations

CHAPTER TWELVE

Tiebreaker Questions, Lists, and Other Fun Stuff

"I have a huge disdain for those artists who say that they don't need a prize to have their talent recognized. If I were a real actress—I'm only an entertainer—I'd do my best to win an Oscar knowing that the Academy is a serious institution of people who really understand about it."

—Carmen Miranda, who was loved but never nominated

THIS SECTION is presented for four major reasons.

REASON #1: You need to learn every single thing there is to know about Oscars because if you're a gay man, some straight people assume that kind of ignorant stereotypical nonsense about us. Well, they do. I don't know why they expect that from gays and not lesbians, but there you are. If you're a lesbian, thank your lucky stars you don't have to deal with this nuttiness from straight men. You can move directly on to Reasons #2, #3, and #4.

But if you're a gay, a straight person will walk right up and ask, "Did Liza Minnelli cohost the year she did *Caberet* or *Arthur*?" (Answer: Neither, it was two years *after Arthur*, as if you didn't know.) And since we were all raised not to disappoint (Sorry, Mom and Dad! Meet my boyfriend!), we like to be able to rise to the occasion.

And by the way, if you're a straight person who has read this far and put up with my comments, I dub you an honorary homosexual here and now. Brava!

REASON #2: You're throwing an Oscar Party—and you need a quick and dirty source of info for tiebreakers should the need arise. With a chapter chock-full of lists such as the one painstakingly supplied next, you can consult it at a glance and come up with a challenge like, "Name the homo who won Best Original Song for *Lion King*." Whoever shouts out "Elton John!" gets the prize for that competition for the Oscar balloting, Name the Movie game, or whatever. And frankly, with a question like that, whoever *doesn't* shout out "Elton John!" should not be invited back next year. But you get the point.

"If I do nothing else, I will convince them that Herbert Stemple knows what won the God-damned Academy Award for Best God-damned Picture of 1955—that's what I'm gonna accomplish."

—John Turturro as Herbie Stemple in *Quiz Show* (1994)

REASON #3: Beyond the need for tiebreakers, there will come a time or two (or 20) during the Oscar telecast when a decided lull in the festivities sets in. To keep that from translating into a lull in *your* party, you need to be prepared with gifts or treats. (See Chapter Five.)

When tiresome commercials come on, or, worse, an Irving Thalberg or Jean Hersholt Humanitarian Award is being shoved at somebody, use this handy-dandy batch of questions to test your guests Oscar I.Q. Whoever answers correctly gets a goodie tossed to them like a performing seal winning a fish. Keep asking questions for as long as the lull lasts. And we all know that when they give some of these people a microphone, it's going be at least 15 minutes we'll never have back again (I'm still recovering from Warren Beatty in 1999), so you'll need plenty of questions and goodies.

REASON #4: Entertainment! Beyond Oscar night, everybody needs something fun for passing the time while passing last night's pizza. Nothing makes better bathroom reading than meaningless facts and information in jolly little bite-sized pieces. Keep this book, stimulating storehouse of Oscar party wisdom and golden treasure-trove that it is, by your toilet. Over time you'll be surprised at how much of its information you acquire. And if worst does come to worst, the publishers assure me that these pages are printed with nonsmudging ink, so if you run out of TP, you have a backup.

Tiebreaker Questions

WHO IS THE ONLY PERSON ACTUALLY NAMED "OSCAR" TO WIN AN OSCAR?
Lyricist Oscar Hammerstein II, who won Best Song (with music by Jerome Kern) for "The Last Time I Saw Paris" from Lady Be Good *(1941) and again four years later (with music by Richard Rodgers) for "It Might As Well Be Spring" from* State Fair *(1945)*

WHAT WAS THE ONLY SILENT FILM TO WIN BEST PICTURE?
Wings *(1927–1928).*

WHAT WAS THE ONLY X-RATED MOVIE EVER TO WIN BEST PICTURE?
Midnight Cowboy *(1969).*

WHAT WAS THE ONLY ANIMATED FILM EVER TO BE NOMINATED FOR BEST PICTURE?
Beauty and the Beast *(1991).*

NAME THE HOMO WHO WON BEST ORIGINAL SONG FOR *THE LION KING.*
Elton John. He could hardly have lost. He was also up for "Hakuna Matata" and "Circle of Life" from the same movie. He won (with lyricist Tim Rice) for "Can You Feel the Love Tonight."

WHO IS THE MOST NOMINATED ACTRESS?
Meryl Streep with 13 nominations, followed by Katharine Hepburn with 12.

WHAT ARE THE ONLY MOVIES THAT WON ALL TOP FIVE (BEST WRITING, DIRECTING, ACTOR, ACTRESS, AND PICTURE) OSCARS?
It Happened One Night *(1934),* One Flew Over The Cuckoo's Nest *(1975),* The Silence of the Lambs *(1991).*

WHO WAS THE FIRST PERSON TO TURN DOWN AN ACADEMY AWARD?
Screenwriter Dudley Nichols turned down his 1935 Best Screenplay Oscar for The Informer *to protest the Academy's attempts to act as a trade arbitrator. Two years later, when the Academy got out of the labor organizing business, Nichols came around and accepted his award. (Oh, and if you said George C. Scott or Marlon Brando, these are the adult questions, not giveaways.)*

WHO IS THE ONLY PERSON TO HAVE WON NOMINATIONS FOR AN OSCAR, TONY, AND EMMY FOR PLAYING THE SAME ROLE?

José Ferrer won the very first Tony Award for his Broadway turn as Cyrano de Bergerac in 1946, and won the Oscar for the film version four years later. He was also nominated for an Emmy for playing Cyrano on television in 1955, but lost that award to Lloyd Nolan playing Captain Queeg in The Caine Mutiny Court Martial.

WHO IS THE ONLY PERSON TO HAVE WON THE OSCAR, TONY, AND EMMY AWARDS IN THE SAME YEAR?

Bob Fosse in 1973, winning the Oscar for Cabaret, *the Tony for* Pippin, *and the Emmy for* Liza With a Z.

WHAT ARE THE ONLY TWO OSCAR-WINNING MOVIES THAT WERE ALSO PULITZER PRIZE–WINNING PLAYS?

You Can't Take It With You *won the Pulitzer for George S. Kaufman and Moss Hart in 1936, and the Best Picture Oscar for Frank Capra's 1938 film adaptation. And* Driving Miss Daisy *won a Pulitzer for Alfred Uhry in 1988 and a Best Screenplay Oscar in 1989. Oh, and did we mention* Driving Miss Daisy *also won the Best Picture Oscar that year?*

WHO ARE THE ONLY TWO WRITERS TO WIN AN OSCAR, TONY, AND A PULITZER PRIZE?

Alfred Uhry and John Patrick Shanley. Uhry won the Oscar for Driving Miss Daisy *in 1989, a Pulitzer for the play version in 1988, and a Tony Award for Best Play in 1997 for* The Last Night of Ballyhoo. *John Patrick Shanley won an Oscar for writing* Moonstruck *and a Tony and Pulitzer Prize for his play* Doubt.

WHO WERE THE ONLY TWO PEOPLE TO WIN BACK-TO-BACK OSCARS FOR DIRECTING?

*John Ford (*The Grapes of Wrath, *1940, and* How Green Was My Valley, *1941) and Joseph L. Mankiewicz (*A Letter to Three Wives, *1949, and* All About Eve, *1950).*

WHO WAS THE ONLY PERSON TO SNAG AN OSCAR WITH A WRITE-IN VOTE?

*Cinematographer Hal Mohr (*A Midsummer Night's Dream, *1936).*

IN WHICH THREE MOVIES WERE THE ENTIRE CASTS NOMINATED FOR ACADEMY AWARDS?

Who's Afraid of Virginia Woolf? *(1966), with Best Actor and Actress nominations for Richard Burton (lost) and Elizabeth Taylor (won), and Best Supporting nominations for George Segal (lost) and Sandy Dennis (won).*

Sleuth *(1972), with Best Actor nominations for Michael Caine and Laurence Olivier (both lost).*

Give 'Em Hell, Harry! *(1975), with a Best Actor nod to James Whitmore (lost).*

WHICH TWO ACTORS HAVE WON BEST ACTOR IN CONSECUTIVE YEARS?

Spencer Tracy for Captains Courageous *(1937)
and* Boys Town *(1938), and Tom Hanks
for* Philadelphia *(1993) and* Forrest
Gump *(1994)*

WHICH TWO ACTRESSES WON CONSECUTIVE BEST ACTRESS AWARDS?

Luise Rainer for The Great Ziegfeld *(1936)
and* The Good Earth *(1937), and Katharine
Hepburn for* Guess Who's Coming to Dinner
(1967) and The Lion in Winter *(1968).*

WHO IS THE ONLY ACTOR TO WIN BEST SUPPORTING ACTOR IN CONSECUTIVE YEARS?

Jason Robards for All the President's Men *(1976)
and* Julia *(1977).*

WHO IS THE ONLY ACTRESS TO WIN BEST SUPPORTING ACTRESS IN CONSECUTIVE YEARS?

Trick question—no actress has.

HOW MANY SEQUELS HAVE WON THE BEST PICTURE?

One, The Godfather, Part II *(1974).*

WHO ARE THE ONLY ACTORS TO WIN OSCARS FOR PLAYING THE SAME CHARACTER?

Marlon Brando in The Godfather *(1972) and Robert DeNiro in* The Godfather, Part II *(1974)—for the role of Vito Corleone .*

WHEN WAS THE FIRST ACADEMY AWARDS CEREMONY?
May 16, 1929, at the Blossom Room of the Holly-wood Roosevelt Hotel.

HOW MUCH WERE THE TICKETS TO THE FIRST OSCAR SHOW?
$10—in today's money around $125.

IN WHAT YEAR WERE THE ACADEMY AWARDS FIRST TELEVISED?
In 1953, in black and white. They were broadcast in color beginning in 1966, and by the mid-1990s, they were broadcast to over 100 countries.

WHO IS THE ONLY ALUMNUS OF *SATURDAY NIGHT LIVE* TO BE NOMINATED FOR AN OSCAR?
Bill Murray was nominated for Best Actor for Lost in Translation *(2003).*

ONE ACTOR APPEARED IN ONLY FIVE MOVIES IN HIS CAREER—EACH OF WHICH WAS A BEST PICTURE NOMINEE. WHO?
*John Cazale (*The Godfather, *1972;* The Conversation, *1974;* The Godfather, Part II, *1974;* Dog Day Afternoon, *1975; and* The Deer Hunter, *1978). All five were nominated for Best Picture,*

and The Godfather, The Godfather, Part II, *and* The Deer Hunter *won. Cazale died from cancer March 12, 1978.*

WHO IS THE ONLY BEST ACTOR WINNER TO HAVE A LOBOTOMY? (YES, *AFTER* HE DID HIS ROLE! SHAME ON YOU.)

Warner Baxter (In Old Arizona, *1928–29). After his Oscar win, his career continued upward until, in 1936, he was named the #1 box-office star. This being Hollywood, you know what happened next—it all went in the crapper tout de suite. He suffered a nervous breakdown and was reduced to appearing in low-budget B movies. Baxter suffered debilitating arthritis at the end of his life, and received a lobotomy in 1951 in what turned out to be a really bad idea to relieve his pain. He died of complications shortly afterward on May 7, 1951.*

WHEN WERE THE ONLY INSTANCES OF A TIE OF AN OSCAR?

Best Actor: 1931–32, Fredric March for Dr. Jekyll and Mr. Hyde *, and Wallace Beery for* The Champ. *Beery had one less vote than March, and rules at the time stated that if anybody came within three votes of the frontrunner, it would be considered a tie.*

Best Actress: 1969, Barbra Streisand for Funny Girl *(1968) and Katharine Hepburn for* The Lion in Winter *(1968).*

Not Quite a Tie: 1961's West Side Story *had cowin-*

ners as directors. Jerome Robbins and Robert Wise split the Best Director Oscar. Catty note— neither one thanked the other in their acceptance speeches. Me-ow!

Q Quiz #1: Just How Much Do You Know About Oscar, Anyway?

1. Trick question—it gets plated with all of them! Copper first, then nickel, to seal the pores of the copper. That's followed by silver, so that the final plating of gold will stick to it better.
2. d. An Oscar is 13½ inches tall.
3. a. An Oscar weighs 8½ pounds.
4. c. They represent the original branches of the Academy.
5. b. Oscar's official name is the Academy Award of Merit.
6. Trick question—it could be either A or C! There are tons of stories floating around about this, but these are the most prevalent. As for B, Bette Davis did tell that story, but she later had to eat her words when the "Oscar" nickname was found in print *three years prior* to when she claimed to have coined it. Oops!

Q Quiz #2: Youngest and Oldest

1. Depends on how you look at it. In 1934, at the age of 6, actress Shirley Temple was awarded a *miniature honorary* Oscar for her

achievements. But if you're talking full-sized Oscars for a specific role, go with Tatum O'Neal, who won Best Supporting Actress for *Paper Moon* (1973) at the tender age of 10. Anna Paquin won Best Supporting Actress for *The Piano* (1993) at age 11.

2. Henry Fonda, 76, for *On Golden Pond* (1981). Due to his bad health he was not present at the awards ceremony so his daughter, Jane Fonda, who also costarred in the film, accepted the award on his behalf. He died five months later.

3. George Burns, at the age of 80, for *The Sunshine Boys* (1975).

QUOTE

"After this I think I'll start taking some of those gentile roles, become the next Robert Redford."

—George Burns, 80, accepting his Best Supporting Actor award for *The Sunshine Boys* (1975)

4. Jessica Tandy, 80, for *Driving Miss Daisy* (1990).

5. Semi-trick question: Groucho Marx was 83 when he received his honorary Oscar statuette at the 46th Annual Academy Awards:

"To Groucho Marx in recognition of his brilliant creativity and for the unequalled achievements of the Marx Brothers in the art of motion picture comedy."

6. Semi-trick question: Myrna Loy was 85 in 1990 when she received her honorary Oscar statuette "in recognition of her extraordinary qualities both onscreen and off, with appreciation for a lifetime's worth of indelible performances."

Q Quiz #3: Shortest and Longest

1. The longest Best Picture winner is *The Lord of the Rings: The Return of the King* (2003) at 250 minutes. *Gone With the Wind* (1939) is the next-longest at 238 minutes.

2. The shortest Best Picture winner is *Marty* (1955) at 91 minutes. The next-shortest is *Annie Hall* (1977), 94 minutes.

3. Anthony Quinn's approximately nine minutes as Paul Gaugin in *Lust for Life* (1956).

4. Beatrice Straight won Best Supporting Actress for less than eight minutes of screen time in *Network* (1976). The next-shortest Oscar-winning performance was Judi Dench for about 10 minutes as Queen Elizabeth in *Shakespeare in Love* (1998).

5. Patty Duke, at the age of 17, in 1963, won Best Supporting Actress for playing the blind and deaf Helen Keller, who, in the climactic scene of *The Miracle Worker*, when she

finally begins to understand spoken language, dramatically utters the word "water."

6. Greer Garson after winning Best Actress for *Mrs. Miniver* (1942). Some unkind reports say that her speech lasted an hour and a half. Can you say "bitter"? It actually clocked in at approximately five and a half minutes. It was after this stunt that a 45-second time limit was imposed.

7. It's a tie. Alfred Hitchcock (winning the Thalberg Award in 1967) and actor William Holden (Best Actor for his role in *Stalag 17*, 1953). Both simply walked up, accepted their awards, said a succinct "Thank you," and walked off.

8. Even though the answer always feels like it had to be the last one, it was actually the 74th Annual Academy Awards held on March 2, 2002. It ran four hours and 23 minutes. Now you know why the producers struggle so hard to keep it close to 3 hours even if it means playing Martin Landau off in the middle of his acceptance speech.

Q Quiz #4: Yes Award/No Award: Actors and Actresses

Glenn Close (No—5 nominations but no win)
Denzel Washington (Yes—5 nominations,
   2 wins: *Glory*, 1989, and *Training Day*, 2001)
Luise Rainer (Yes—won for *The Great Ziegfeld*,
   1936, and *The Good Earth*, 1937)

Peter O'Toole (No—7 nominations, but no win; did get an honorary award in 2002)

Tom Cruise (No—3 nominations but no win)

Whoopi Goldberg (Yes—2 nominations, and won for *Ghost*, 1990)

Jim Carrey (No—never nominated)

Harrison Ford (No—1 nomination, but no win)

Morgan Freeman (Yes—4 nominations, and won for *Million Dollar Baby*, 2004)

Ronald Reagan (No—never nominated)

Judy Garland (Yes—but a trick question. Won a *special miniature* statuette for her performances that year as a juvenile in 1939, which included *The Wizard of Oz*. Nominated twice more, in 1954 and 1961, but did not win.)

Ernest Borgnine (Yes—1 nomination, won for *Marty*, 1959)

Bette Midler (No—2 nominations but no win)

Meg Ryan (No—never nominated)

Anna Magnani (Yes—2 nominations, and won for *The Rose Tattoo*, 1955)

Debra Winger (No—3 nominations, but no win)

Sean Connery (Yes—1 nomination, won for *The Untouchables*, 1987)

Albert Finney (No—5 nominations, but no win)

Angela Lansbury (No—3 nominations, no win)

Benicio del Toro (Yes—2 nominations, and won for *Traffic*, 2000)

Richard Burton (No—7 nominations, but no win)

Faye Dunaway (Yes—3 nominations, and won for *Network*, 1976)

Helena Bonham Carter (No—1 nomination,
   but no win)
Judi Dench (Yes—5 nominations, and won for
   Shakespeare in Love, 1998)
Madeline Kahn (No—2 nominations, but no
   win)
Peter Sellers (No—2 nominations, but no win)
Bing Crosby (Yes—won for *Going My Way*, 1944)
Ginger Rogers (Yes—1 nomination, won for
   Kitty Foyle, 1940)
Fred Astaire (Yes—but a trick question: 1 acting
   nomination, for *Towering Inferno*, 1974, but
   received a special Oscar for "his unique
   artistry and contribution to the technique of
   musical pictures" in 1949)

Q Quiz #5: Yes Award/No Award— Directors

D. W. Griffith (No—but honorary award in
   1935)
Victor Fleming (Yes—1 nomination, and won
   for *Gone With the Wind*, 1939)
James Ivory (No—3 nominations, but no win)
George Lucas (No—2 nominations, but no win;
   Thalberg Award in 1991)
John Ford (Yes—5 nominations, and won for
   The Informer (1935), *The Grapes of Wrath*
   (1940), *How Green Was My Valley* (1941),
   and *The Quiet Man* (1952)
Otto Preminger (No—2 directing nominations,
   but no win)

Elia Kazan (Yes—5 nominations, won for *Gentleman's Agreement*, 1947, and *On the Waterfront*, 1954)

Lina Wertmüller (No—1 nomination, no win)

Martin Scorsese (No—5 directing nominations, but no win)

Ron Howard (Yes—1 nomination, and a win for *A Beautiful Mind*, 2001)

Stanley Kubrick (No—4 directing nominations, but no win)

Fritz Lang (No—never nominated)

Spike Lee (No—no directing nomination)

Vincente Minnelli (Yes—2 nominations, won for *Gigi*, 1958)

Jane Campion (No—1 directing nomination, but no win)

David Lean (Yes—7 nominations, won for *Bridge on the River Kwai*, 1957, and *Lawrence of Arabia*, 1962)

Woody Allen (Yes—6 nominations, won for *Annie Hall*, 1977)

QUOTE

"When the Academy called, I panicked. I thought they might want their Oscars back and the pawn shop has been out of business for a while."

—Woody Allen, presenting at the 73rd Annual Academy Awards

Federico Fellini (No—but an honorary award
in 1992)

Cecil B. DeMille (No—1 directing nomination,
but no win; honorary award in 1949 and a
Thalberg in 1952)

Alfred Hitchcock (No—5 nominations, but no
win; Thalberg Award in 1967)

Frank Capra (Yes—6 nominations, won for *It
Happened One Night*, 1937; *Mr. Deeds Goes
to Town*, 1936; and *You Can't Take It With
You*, 1938)

Sofia Coppola (No—1 nomination, but no win)

Billy Wilder (Yes—8 nominations, and won for
The Lost Weekend, 1945, and *The Apartment*,
1960)

Sam Mendes (Yes—1 nomination, and a win for
American Beauty, 1999)

QUOTE

"Screw the Oscars. Screw the
Academy Awards. Screw *me*,
Sidney. Please. *Please*!"

—Maggie Smith as movie actress
Diana Barrie to her gay husband
(played by Michael Caine) after her
character lost the Oscar in *California
Suite* (1978)—ironically, the role that
won Maggie Smith a real Oscar!

THE FINAL WORD:

Cut, Print, That's a Wrap!